"From the time I picked up *Guilt-* to put it down. Every single page i as I found the book powerful and the point, every page is power-pac

—**Christine Abraham,** founder of Bible Cafe

"Finally, there is a book that helps us understand that we don't need to feel shame about our crazy lives and the way we seek God in real-life moments. Emily Ryan's *Guilt-Free Quiet Times* is the bondage-breaking book that women need! If you have ever felt that pit in your stomach about being inconsistent or bewildered about having time with the Lord, get ready to find freedom from the myths that have been holding you back."

—**Amber Lia,** devoted quiet-time momma of four sons and best-selling author

"Like Saint George valiantly slaying the dragon, Emily Ryan confronts the destructive myths that keep many of us from having the personal time with the Lord that we desire. *Guilt-Free Quiet Times* will help you seek the Lord in your own way, in your own time. Read it more than once. Buy copies for your friends. I already know what I'll be giving as Christmas gifts this year!"

—**Shirley Raye Redmond,** author of *Courageous World Changers,* winner of the 2021 *Christianity Today* Book Award for Children and Youth

"For every myth we believe about spending time with God, Emily Ryan weaves biblical truths, personal testimonies, practical applications, and reflections to help us reframe our narratives about 'quiet time.' She skillfully balances laugh-out-loud humor with revelatory aha moments when comparing our picture of quiet time to the truth of where, when, and how God meets His children."

—**Casey Hilty,** speaker and author of *Her Children Arise*

"As someone who continues to recover from a legalistic background, I found this book refreshing in its biblical approach to exposing myths that often hinder our desire to spend time with God. If you're ready to unlock the chains of guilt, shame, and the constant feeling of failure and enjoy your time with God again, *Guilt-Free Quiet Times* will take you by the hand and walk with you toward the freedom that is yours in Christ Jesus."

—**Cathy Baker,** founder of Creative Pauses

"Emily Ryan's words step into our traditional quiet-time stories like a gentle midwife, leading us out of the land of expectations into the fullness of life Jesus set us free to enjoy. If I had to choose one book to gift to a new believer or a worn-out saint, I'd pick *Guilt-Free Quiet Times.*"

—**Janet Newberry,** author, speaker, podcaster, and consultant

"Prepare to have God get your attention in an unexpected, personal way. I'm nearing my eighth decade, and little surprises me any longer. This book did. I've read through the Bible every year for ages, but there were fresh insights in this small treasure of a volume. This is a book to savor and to share."

—**Shirley E. Leonard,** author of *With Each Passing Moment*

guilt-free quiet times

7 Myths about Your Devotional Time with God

EMILY E. RYAN

Our Daily Bread
Publishing.

Requests for permission to quote from this book should be directed to: Permissions Department, Our Daily Bread Publishing, PO Box 3566, Grand Rapids, MI 49501, or contact us by email at permissionsdept@odb.org.

Published in association with Books & Such Literary Management, 52 Mission Circle, Suite 122, PMB 170, Santa Rosa, CA 95409-5370, www.booksandsuch.com.

Interior design by Michael J. Williams

Library of Congress Cataloging-in-Publication Data

Names: Ryan, Emily E., author.
Title: Guilt-free quiet times : 7 myths about your devotional time with God / Emily E. Ryan.
Description: Grand Rapids, MI : Our Daily Bread Publishing, 2024. | Summary: "Offers readers a fresh vision for integrating time with God into the rhythms--and amid the realities and responsibilities--of a woman's everyday life by humorously debunking 7 myths about the so-called requirements for quiet times. Includes discussion questions for women's retreats, book clubs, or Bible studies" -- Provided by publisher.
Identifiers: LCCN 2024000064 (print) | LCCN 2024000065 (ebook) | ISBN 9781640703278 (paperback) | ISBN 9781640703285 (epub)
Subjects: LCSH: Christian women--Prayers and devotions. | Time--Religious aspects--Christianity. | Devotional exercises.
Classification: LCC BV4844 .R89 2024 (print) | LCC BV4844 (ebook) | DDC 242/.643--dc23/eng/20240216
LC record available at https://lccn.loc.gov/2024000064
LC ebook record available at https://lccn.loc.gov/2024000065

Printed in the United States of America
24 25 26 27 28 29 30 31 / 8 7 6 5 4 3 2 1

To every woman longing for relationship over religion,
prayer over performance, and honesty over hypocrisy,
and to those brave enough to share their stories first

Sometimes hallway church chats make the best sermons.

Contents

What Is a Quiet Time?

Quiet time is a popular term used to describe the time a person sets aside to communicate with God. Common elements of a quiet time may include praying, reading a devotion, reading the Bible, meditating, and journaling.

While the benefits and necessity of time with the Lord are evident throughout Scripture, the expression *quiet time* does not actually appear in the Bible.

Introduction

The Fine Print

Y ou're probably reading this because your desire to have consistent, effective time with the Lord has been met with resistance. There's a significant gap between where you want to be and where you are, so you're looking for the answer, formula, or perfect checklist that will catapult your quiet times from dull to divine.

You won't find it here.

This book is not meant to tell you what to do. Rather, it's meant to give you permission not to do certain things. Things that, until now, you may have thought were as pivotal and nonnegotiable as salvation itself.

When you have a project or a goal, many times your to-do list isn't nearly as important as your not-to-do list. For example, if you want to wake up early to exercise, the success of that goal begins with your decision not to stay up late the night before. Intentionally saying no to things that don't matter makes it easier for you to say yes to the things that really do matter.

When it comes to your time with the Lord, you need to say no to some things as well.

You need to say no to legalism or rigidity.

You need to say no to someone else's magic formula that works perfectly for him or her but creates chaos and guilt in your own life.

You need to say no to walking through the motions.

You need to say no to Satan's lie that it's all or nothing.

That's why it's so important to expose the myths that have surfaced regarding quiet times. Without the right motives, of course, you could read this book and interpret it as permission to spend as little time with God as possible. But the goal is not to give you an excuse to do less. The goal is to give you the freedom and empowerment to do more.

Freedom to chase after God in your own unique and energizing way.

Freedom to stumble.

Freedom to accept the grace He offers.

Freedom to get to know God himself rather than get to know how to have a perfect quiet time.

If you've ever fallen in love, or observed others who have, you know that no two love stories—and therefore no two relationships—are exactly alike. Some begin quickly and suddenly. Others grow slowly and gradually over time. Some couples never spend a day apart. Others must navigate demanding schedules, challenging seasons, or temporary long-distance separation due to work or deployment. What makes love so special is not that it's predictable and ordinary but that it's intimately unique to each couple.

Your relationship with God is a love story as well, and my prayer is that this book will help you as you fall deeper in love with Him.

You'll find suggestions and tips in the chapters that follow. You'll find inspiration. You'll even find a little humor. But above all, you'll find grace.

May the Lord meet you, wherever you are and however He desires, and draw you closer to Him.

~ Emily

Your Quiet Time
Must Be Quiet

Shh . . . By all means, turn off that ruckus! You will not hear God if YouTube is too loud. And while you're at it, silence Alexa, mute your phone, muzzle your dog, disconnect your smoke detector, and make sure the dishwasher isn't running. You don't want any noise to distract you from the voice of God. If there must be noise, the only acceptable sounds are nature-related ones because God created nature for us to enjoy. Birds chirping. Waves crashing. Wind blowing. These are all fine. (But not crickets, of course, because crickets chirp at night, and the perfect quiet time is in the morning. So sorry, no cricket noises.)

TRUTH: God does not need silence to be heard. He whispers to us through our hearts, not our ears.

What Happens in Vegas

Few things are louder than Las Vegas hotel lobbies. I was reminded of that when my friend Betsy and I tagged along on a senior trip our friend Angie had planned for her daughter Elena. One of Elena's favorite bands was performing for one weekend only in the- city- that- never- sleeps, so the four of us—one eighteen-year-old and three moms—booked a weekend away.

I'm often the first one awake on girls' trips, so I'm used to tiptoeing out of a hotel room like a ninja, careful not to disturb my roommates, and finding free coffee and quiet in a secluded corner of the lobby while waiting for my friends to wake up. On the last morning of our Vegas trip, I found neither.

Instead, when the elevator opened to the first floor, I was greeted by the same frat-party noises, lights, and smells as the night before. An invisible hint of beer lingered in the air like

15

smoke after fireworks. Lights flickered and flashed, pulsing with strobing patterns in a rainbow of neon colors. Slot machines were alive and angered.

Nothing about this morning was quiet.

After paying too much for coffee, I found an open bistro table that hugged the side of the main walkway and settled in with my digital Bible. For over an hour, I sat in non-silence with God. Thinking. Praying. Journaling. Listening. On the outside, my ears heard every whir and hum. On the inside, my heart heard my Lord.

When my friends finally texted that they were awake, I returned to the hotel room with my heart at rest, thankful I could still hear God above the noise and nonsense of the world.

Your Ears versus Your Heart

I imagine King David bears a little responsibility for the idea that all of our time with the Lord must be peaceful and quiet. After all, when he wrote the famous Twenty-Third Psalm, he describes the ideal atmosphere. Green pastures, quiet waters, surrounded by soft, fluffy sheep. Who wouldn't feel close to God in such a peaceful, calm, quiet setting?

We forget, however, that the young shepherd who sought the Lord in quiet pastures grew up to be a great king who sought the Lord in noisy battles.

Nevertheless, the expectation that our quiet time must be, well, *quiet*, persists. It's the number-one unspoken rule of spending time with God, reinforced by the very terminology we use.

But what if life is loud? What if the day gets rowdy? Does God tap His foot like an impatient kindergarten teacher, pursing His lips and muttering, "I'll wait. I can wait *all* day if I have to," until the last whisper gets snuffed out like a candle?

Of course not. The call of quiet is for our benefit, not His. And while it's true that times of serenity and peace are ideal for spending time with Him, we must be careful not to become so dependent on the silence of the atmosphere that we are unable to hear Him in times of chaos.

Let's face it. Life is crazy. If we wait until every single noise or distraction is eliminated before we can spend time with the Lord, chances are, the opportunity may never present itself. Children will cry. The phone will ring. People will laugh and talk and interrupt and argue. It is downright impossible to silence every single sound around us, so what becomes more important is the stillness of our hearts.

Is your heart listening?

Forget about your ears. Forget about the noise. Forget about the hums and echoes and jingles and thuds.

What does your heart hear?

When your heart is listening for the quiet whisper of the Lord, you can hear Him in the midst of any wind, earthquake, fire, or Vegas soundscape the world throws your way.

Embracing the Noise

In some seasons, especially seasons with young children at home, quiet moments are a luxury. A rare luxury. Your home is not a hushed haven. Instead, it's a circus, and you are the ringmaster. To imply that it must be completely silent for an intimate connection with God would be like throwing you into water and demanding that you remain dry.

In these cases, rather than fighting the noise, consider embracing it for a change. The book of Mark tells about people trying to bring little children to Jesus in order for Him to bless them. Jesus's disciples rebuked the people and tried to send the children away. They didn't think Jesus should be bothered by their rowdiness. Jesus, however, adamantly disagreed. "Let the little children come to me, and do not hinder them" (10:14), He said. "And he took the children in his arms, placed his hands on them and blessed them" (v. 16).

For a mother or grandmother with young children around, I don't think there is a more liberating passage. No longer are you obligated to stockpile energy for that magic hour when your kids are finally asleep, your husband is finally settled with his TV and remote, and the house is finally still. Instead, you're free to wrap your pajama-clad kids up in a blanket, cuddle with them on the couch, and spend time with God together during family or bedtime devotions.

I began doing this with my own kids when my oldest was about six months old, and it took numerous forms over the years. I read the Bible out loud during bath time. I used their Awana books to memorize Scripture with them. We piled all four kids on the floor and talked about God's many blessings. We prayed together, sang songs together, and read so many versions of baby Moses in a basket that I even discovered a mistake in one of our children's Bibles.

I'm not going to lie. Those times rarely resulted in picture-perfect moments in which they all knelt by the bed in order from oldest to youngest and recited the Lord's Prayer by heart. Most times our discussions involved commentary on dinosaurs or bottoms or grandparents or Cinderella. And many of our prayers were seasoned with outbursts of "Sit down!" or "Stop that!" or "You're supposed to be praying not licking your sister!"

But even in those moments, I was sensitive to God's presence. Even in the chaos, I heard Him speaking, and no matter how loud my children could be, I learned that God can be even louder.

Experimenting with Sound

Music, also, can be an effective and powerful addition to your "quiet" times. Consider how many of the psalms were written to be, in essence, musical prayers. David himself said he would "sacrifice with shouts of joy" and "sing and make music to the LORD" (Psalm 27:6).

It's not even necessary to be musical in order to embrace music. You don't need to be able to match pitch, only to make a "joyful noise." That means you are free to sing along with the radio, clap your hands, shake a tambourine, or turn your kitchen counter into a drum.

Most of us feel comfortable incorporating music into our Sunday morning worship time at church, but we never think to use it in our living rooms. But in the Bible, we see God's people spontaneously erupt in song as an authentic response to God's hand upon their lives. On the battlefield. In the desert. Before deliverance. After finding water. In prayer and praise. In sorrow and joy. Music is one of the most authentic forms of worship we see displayed in the lives of those in love with the Lord, so there's no reason why it should be set aside for corporate worship alone.

Faith Comes by Hearing

Another way to experiment with sound in your "quiet" time is by listening to the Word of God instead of reading it. Paul explains in Romans that "faith comes by hearing, and hearing by the word of God" (10:17 NKJV).

With the plethora of printed Bibles available today, we forget that the Word of God was originally passed from generation to generation orally. People didn't have eleven Bibles on their bookshelves. They didn't have online bookstores at their fingertips. Instead, they had the priests, the prophets, and their own family members to tell them about God.

So perhaps one of the most powerful things you can do is close your Bible.

Yes, you read that correctly. Just close it, lay it on your nightstand, and don't read it for a few days.

Instead, *listen* to it.

There are countless audio Bibles available, and you can find them at bookstores and libraries or online or via mobile apps. Versions range from single narrators to full-fledged audio dramas complete with sound effects and multiple actors reading various parts.

When you open yourself up to the spoken Word of God, suddenly you can hear the Lord, literally, in your car, your kitchen, your laundry room, or your gym. Familiar stories become new and exciting. Familiar passages take on new meanings. You may even notice emphases and inflections you never caught before, and—my personal favorite benefit—you never have to stumble over hard-to-pronounce words and names again.

Scripture Memory Music

One final suggestion for incorporating sound into your times with the Lord involves combining both music and the oral Word of God. If you've ever tried to memorize Scripture, you probably know how difficult it can be. It takes effort, time, and a whole lot of concentration. And yet, for those inevitable times when the world chatters in your ear like an incessant toddler and pure quiet is elusive, memorized verses hidden deep in the corners of your heart work as God's megaphone to your soul.

Thankfully, music makes memorizing Scripture much easier.

For some reason, we are quite used to this concept when it comes to teaching our children the Word of God, but we forget that it can be just as effective for adults. If memorizing Scripture is something you'd like to incorporate into your time with the Lord (and I highly recommend it), find some songs that have Bible verses set to music. Search online for "Scripture memory music," or go to your local Christian bookstore and ask for recommendations. And remember, sometimes children's songs will be your best resource, so don't forget to explore the kids' section.

Finally, remember that God's whisper is louder than the world's shouts. If your heart is listening, you can hear Him in the middle of a rock concert, a child's birthday party, a football stadium, or even a Vegas casino.

DEVOTIONAL MOMENTS FROM THE BIBLE

The Crowd Shouts "Hosanna"
Matthew 21; Mark 11; Luke 19; John 12

On the Sunday before His death, Jesus and His disciples traveled to Jerusalem for the annual Passover celebration. As they neared the road that goes down the Mount of Olives into the city, a crowd gathered to welcome Him. Hungry for help and desperate for deliverance, they hoped Jesus was the political savior they had been waiting for. A future king who would liberate them from Roman oppression and restore the glory of Israel.

As word spread, the crowd grew, and their enthusiasm could not be contained. They waved palm branches high in the air for Jesus to see, greeting Him as they would a king returning from victory on the battlefield.

With each step, the energy swelled as the cheers and shouts from the crowd grew louder and louder. "Hosanna!" they cried out with joy. "Hosanna to the Son of

David! Blessed is he who comes in the name of the Lord!" (Matthew 21:9).

But as the boisterous crowd waved their palm branches and spread their cloaks on the road before Jesus in an act of honor and submission, another group watched from the sidelines in disgust. The Pharisees, the religious leaders of the day, did not approve of the crowd's riotous display of devotion. It lacked propriety. It lacked decorum. How could Jesus allow such a blatant disregard for order and civility? How dare He accept their messianic exclamations? Had He no respect for the Scriptures?

The Pharisees tried to shout over the crowd. "Teacher, rebuke your disciples!" (Luke 19:39) they called to Jesus. Their bold command seemed to suggest that if Jesus were truly worthy of the crowd's worship, surely He would put the mob in its place, command a holy hush, and return peace and quiet to the land.

If ever Jesus smirked, I imagine this was the moment. He was energized by the noise, not annoyed by it. Blessed, not bothered. The cries from the crowd were genuine shouts of praise, something the Pharisees knew nothing about. He turned to them and shook His head. "I tell you," Jesus said, "if they keep quiet, the stones will cry out" (Luke 19:40).

Don't let a simple rise in decibels keep you from spending time with Jesus, and don't let stones cry out in your place. Jesus hears hearts through every other sound.

Real Women, Real Stories

Jamie—No Fancy Plan

I have a hard time just being quiet. Someone once told me a proper quiet time begins by sitting still for sixty seconds. No talking or praying. Just being still and open to listening. This hasn't worked well for me at all. I can get about ten seconds in, then something pops in my mind and I'm completely distracted.

My mind runs like crazy so it's very difficult for me to avoid tangents and actually focus. Because of this, I unload any and everything to Jesus in prayer as it comes to mind. No fancy plan. No rhyme or reason. It's more of a crash course in needing the Lord, knowing He hears everything, and laying every struggle at His feet.

Julie—Busy Hands

I often hear best from God when my hands are busy—doing dishes, driving, pulling weeds, even in the shower. For some reason a mindless task helps me focus better than trying to sit quietly and listen. I've learned to embrace my unique style of listening for God rather than feel guilty or bad for not being traditional.

Janet—Right-Hand Turns

My favorite time with God is during my hourlong commute to work. I have developed a rhythm to the commute that I follow as I drive. First, I begin with a prayer of gratitude for the day and all that it holds, then pray about anything else that pops into my mind. After that, I transition to listening to and singing along with uplifting praise and worship music for twenty to thirty minutes. About that time, I make a right-hand turn that places me on the Blue Ridge Parkway. This leg of my commute is a winding twenty-five-minute drive at forty-five miles per hour viewing the beauty of God's creation the entire way. I turn down the music and continue my conversation with God. In the quiet, I cover myself, my loved ones, friends, and coworkers in prayer and offer other prayers of petition and gratitude. When I make another right-hand turn to exit the parkway, I turn the music back up. Once again, I am worshiping and singing along.

Mary Helen—*The Psalms in Silence*

When I was in graduate school, I took a class on the Psalms that was taught by a Catholic priest. He required us to spend twenty minutes a day in total silence with just our Bible and a journal. We didn't have to share what we'd written, but we did have to record our time and show that we had completed the assignment. Sometimes, he would assign specific psalms for us to read. Other times, we could pick our own.

Because it was a class requirement, it was easy to try something different, and it helped me develop that routine of sitting in silence, reading, praying, and journaling. I don't get to do that much anymore, but I miss it, and I often think I should get back to it.

Now I read a short devotion before I go to bed most nights. It centers my mind and calms me down to read something positive before I go to sleep. I also think of five good things that happened that day and thank God for them. It's not as much as it used to be, but it keeps me grounded and focused on Him.

Stephanie—The Bible Recap

I was all over the place with my quiet time until I found a Bible app that reads to me and *The Bible Recap* podcast with Tara-Leigh Cobble [Cobble's resources walk Bible readers through a chronological one-year reading plan with engaging and easy-to-understand daily summaries]. I am usually a visual learner, but the audio aspect has really helped me. I listen every morning when I wake up and get ready to work out. Most days I go on a walk after my daily workout video. This has become a wonderful time for me to pray and listen to God in the peace of the early morning and stillness of the darkness.

Guilt-Free Ideas for More

1. Pray aloud.
2. Listen to the Psalms. Try putting your favorite passages to music and create a special song just for you and the Lord.
3. Speak openly to the Lord with your children by acknowledging His blessings (even the small ones) as they come throughout the day.
4. Immerse yourself in nature and listen to the sounds that God has created.
5. Access a playlist of Scripture memory music and listen to it every day for a week. If you have children, invite them to listen with you.
6. Play praise music while you're folding laundry and sing along.
7. Listen to all two and a half hours of Handel's Messiah. Per tradition, stand in worship during the "Hallelujah Chorus."
8. If you live near the ocean, drive to the beach and meet with God at the edge of the water. Close your eyes and let the sound of the waves remind you of God's power.
9. Listen to instrumental versions of your favorite hymns.
10. Declare your bathroom a "no phone zone." Use whatever moments of quiet you have in that room to pray or memorize Scripture.

Reflect and Discuss

1. In general, how much of your day is usually quiet?
2. Do you find it difficult or easy to talk to God when you're surrounded by noise? Why?
3. How have you incorporated music or other sounds into your time with the Lord?
4. What would it look like to invite your children, spouse, friends, or others to your quiet times?
5. What idea from this chapter are you most excited to try?

Your Quiet Time Must Be Thirty Minutes Long

Keep going! The first twenty-nine minutes of your quiet time don't really count. If you stop just shy of thirty minutes, it's like running a marathon and quitting before you cross the finish line. You must keep going. If you're a new Christian, or if you're just beginning to have a daily quiet time, you are allowed a short grace period in which fifteen- or twenty-minute quiet times are acceptable. But they are like using a 5K or 10K to train for a marathon. You are expected to build on the length of your quiet times until you reach the ultimate goal of regular thirty-minute quiet times. If, after thirty minutes, God is still speaking to you, politely tell Him that His time is up and that He'll have to finish the conversation tomorrow.

TRUTH: Let the Holy Spirit, not the clock, determine the length of time you spend with the Lord.

Moment of Silence

My heart beat against my chest like a scorned lover banging on a locked door. Insistent. Persistent. Relentless and rude.

My ears struggled to block out the relentless ticking of the clock that seemed to echo against the walls of my classroom.

Every breath was shallow and stifled. Every appendage fidgeted with fear.

And then the bell rang. The students came in, and the principal's voice from the intercom led us in the pledge and the daily moment of silence.

For the first few months of my first semester as a public school teacher, my most authentic moments with God came not during perfectly planned, well-executed quiet times, but rather during those daily principal-led moments of silence when I closed my eyes, practiced focus breathing, and begged God for the panic attacks to stop.

Inhale *Jesus*.

Exhale *Help*.

For weeks, it was all I could manage. Just a breath. Just a moment.

But it was enough.

The Perfect Number of Minutes

I don't know which version of the myth you've heard—maybe it's thirty minutes, maybe ten, maybe even an hour—but you'll be happy to know that the Bible never mentions a "magic" number of minutes for you to spend with God each day.

If anything, it cautions against watching the clock. In His most famous sermon ever, the Sermon on the Mount, Jesus tells us clearly, "When you pray, do not keep on babbling like pagans, for they think they will be heard because of their many words" (Matthew 6:7). Other versions, such as the English Standard Version and the Amplified Bible, describe this as using "empty phrases" or "meaningless repetition," concentrating on quantity or volume instead of quality.

But still, somewhere in the unspoken rules of churchdom, we've created a mystical, quantifiable goal that spending *x* amount of minutes with God per day is a requirement.

As if any number of minutes is actually enough.

If you want to know the perfect number of minutes a day to spend with God, I'll tell you:

All of them.

After all, that's the highest goal, isn't it? To spend every single moment in constant communication with God.

That's not to say that dedicated, concentrated time with the

Lord isn't important. It is. But when you become intentional about speaking with God and listening to Him through the Holy Spirit throughout the day, you begin to feel less pressure to "get it all in" during your quiet time. The concentrated times you spend with Him simply become deeper continuations of a conversation that never really stops, rather than awkward, forced conversations monitored by a timer, alarm clock, or stopwatch.

A Warning against Punching the Clock

You may recall the story of Eutychus in Acts 20. He was a man present at a house where Paul was preaching in Troas. Paul knew he was leaving the next day, and he wanted to fit everything in before he left, so he kept talking on and on until midnight. Eutychus, bless his heart, was tired. So tired, in fact, that he fell asleep while sitting in a window of the third story and fell out the window to the ground below.

Don't worry. Paul put his hands on him and Eutychus was raised from the dead, but the whole story makes you wonder. If our goal in spending time with God, whether in our quiet time, at church, or during any other situation, is merely to clock in and clock out again, we're missing the point.

Our goal should not be connecting with God for a random, predetermined length of time. Our goal should be to remain so connected to God that time becomes irrelevant.

Talk Is Cheap

In Ecclesiastes, we're advised to let our words be few. "As you enter the house of God, keep your ears open and your mouth shut. . . . Don't make rash promises, and don't be hasty in bringing matters before God. After all, God is in heaven, and you are here on earth. So let your words be few. Too much activity gives you restless dreams; too many words make you a fool. . . . Talk is cheap, like daydreams and other useless activities. Fear God instead" (Ecclesiastes 5:1–3, 7 NLT).

The message here is not that it's wrong to spend a lot of time talking with God. The message is that the time we spend *following* God is more important than the time we spend making promises to Him. We could spend four hours a day talking with God, but if we aren't obeying Him for the remaining twenty hours a day, our time with Him is meaningless.

Consider the parable of the two sons Jesus relates in Matthew 21. A man told both of his sons to go out into the vineyard and work. The first one said he wouldn't go, but then later changed his mind and followed his father's request (v. 29). The second son told his father he would go, but he never did (v. 30). Which son was obedient? Not the son who spent time making promises to his father, but the son who did as his father instructed.

If you fill your quiet time with nothing more than rituals, empty words, or meaningless prayers, then thirty minutes (or ten minutes, or an hour) will never be enough. On the other hand, if you take time to align your will to His through a simple, heartfelt prayer, it may be enough for the moment.

How to Pray Always

Time becomes a factor again, however, when you consider Paul's command to the Thessalonians. "Rejoice always, pray continually, give thanks in all circumstances; for this is God's will for you in Christ Jesus" (1 Thessalonians 5:16–18).

Other versions say, "pray without ceasing" (NKJV), "pray constantly" (RSV), and "never stop praying" (NLT).

Seriously? Never. Stop. Praying. Like, *ever*?

That thirty-minute quiet time isn't looking so difficult anymore, is it? Is that even a realistic command? And if so, how do you do it? How do you pray without ceasing if you can't even have a ten-minute quiet time (much less a five-minute shower) without being interrupted or disturbed?

The key is to understand that our communication with God does not have to end whenever we say amen. I used to think prayer was something that had to have a formal, official beginning, like, "Dear Lord," and a perfect, official ending, like, "In Jesus's name, amen." Now I understand that prayer can sometimes be more like sending God a text message than mailing Him a letter.

There are moments when you don't have time for long, wordy prayers to God. You're in the trenches. You're at the end of your rope. You're in the middle of life and just can't push the pause button.

Other times, you couldn't formulate a prayer even if you had all the time in the world. Your mind feels like a spider web. Your emotions are pulling you down like quicksand. Your heart lies broken on the ground, and everyone you know seems to be stomping on the pieces.

We've all been there. Your heart wants to talk to God, but the chaos and noise of the moment don't allow for "pretty" prayers. Those are the times when you need something you can whisper in a single breath. Something concise. Something that can hold you over until you can gather your thoughts, get away, and spend quality time with God.

In addition to the desperate-but-effective prayer I mentioned earlier—inhale *Jesus* and exhale *Help*—I also use simple, five-word prayers like, "Not my timing, but yours," when I need to quickly align myself with God. Uncomplicated prayers from a person whose heart is bent toward God can be just as powerful as the longer, poetic prayers of David. They're not meant to altogether replace dedicated, prayer-closet quiet times that you spend talking with God. But they can be an extremely powerful way to bridge the gap in between.

You will experience the most spiritual growth from your one-on-one time with God, just like your friendships will grow deeper over face-to-face coffee dates. But for those times when it's impossible to connect on that level, or it's not practical to have a perfect, lengthy quiet time, it's still possible to touch base with God through a whisper.

Five-Word Prayers to Whisper in the Moment

Not my *will*, but yours.	*When you need to submit to God's sovereignty.*
Not my *timing*, but yours.	*When God seems to be moving too quickly or too slowly.*
Not my *day*, but yours.	*When you want to dedicate your day to Him.*
Not my *reason*, but yours.	*When you don't understand why but want to trust God anyway.*
Not my *stuff*, but yours.	*When you struggle with finances or material things.*
Not my *way*, but yours.	*When you need to trust God with the journey and not just the destination.*
Not my *job*, but yours.	*When you need to remember that only God can change someone's heart.*
Not my *glory*, but yours.	*When you are overcome with His blessings.*

A Criminal with Three Seconds to Eternity
Luke 23:32–43

Sentenced to death by crucifixion, the unnamed man was one of three to be executed that day. After the man was dragged to a place known as *Golgotha* or *Skull Hill*, Roman centurions with angry eyes and calloused hands nailed him to a wooden cross with iron spikes as long as the soldier's hand. The agony was torturous.

Beside him was a man he'd probably only heard about named Jesus. In his muddled mind distracted by pain, he almost certainly couldn't imagine why Jesus was here. He wasn't a criminal like him. He didn't have the reputation of a hardened thief or a malicious murderer. From the little he'd heard, the thief probably knew Jesus was a kind teacher. Some in the crowd even seemed to be weeping for Him.

Perhaps the man blinked away the sweat and scanned the mob below for anyone who might be weeping for him as well. If so, he likely found no one.

On the other side of Jesus, the third convict began shouting, hurling insults at Jesus and provoking Him with curses. "Aren't you the Messiah?" he taunted. "Save yourself and us!" (Luke 23:39).

The man heard the criminal's insults and waited for Jesus to respond, but no words came. At last, he could take it no longer. "Don't you fear God?" he yelled to his fellow felon. "We're all about to die! The difference is that you and I are getting the punishment we deserve. But this man—he's not like us. He's done nothing wrong!" (Luke 23:40–41, author's paraphrase).

As he hung there, struggling and fighting for breath, the man may have wondered which was worse—the excruciating pain or the unbearable weight of his guilt. Surely his body ached for death to relieve him of this agony, but deep within his spirit, his soul still longed for life.

I imagine the man averting his eyes and fixing his gaze on the innocent man beside him. In perhaps the shortest devotional moment ever recorded in the Bible, he cried out to Jesus as best he could. "Jesus, remember me when you come into your kingdom" (v. 42).

Jesus must have turned His head toward him and blinked away the blood and tears before answering. In that moment, there was no mob. No Roman centurions. No other criminal. No weeping disciples. There was only them, and a promise that passed between their wooden crosses and settled into eternity. "Today," Jesus responded, "you will be with me in paradise" (Luke v. 43).

When the depth of a moment with Jesus is genuine, the length matters not.

Real Women, Real Stories

Jane—Minute by Minute

After my divorce, my mother tried to help me by giving me some Bible verses written out on paper. I ripped them up and threw them back at her. God hadn't healed my marriage. Why would I trust Him to heal my heart?

It took a long time, probably four or five years, for me to come back to Jesus. I slowly understood that I'd been leaning on my mom's faith my whole life rather than growing on my own. No wonder I'd been shaken when my marriage ended.

God drew me back to Him in baby steps. No big revelations

or life-changing moments. It was more minute by minute than day by day. I'd hear a song that spoke to my heart or a word of advice from my pastor. Sometimes it would be a Bible verse from a friend at just the right moment.

In time, God not only healed my heart, but He also used that time to show me that's how my brain works. I'm not a "big moment" kind of person. I'm not one to do long, in-depth Bible studies or to follow elaborate reading plans. I'm way too all over the map for long, focused meditation.

Instead, I need that minute by minute reminder of who God is and who I am in Christ. Now, I intentionally set up those reminders so I'll get them throughout the day. I subscribe to devotional emails that I get at work. I journal when I need to clear my head, sometimes in the middle of the day. I use the Bible app for short nuggets of truth that can get me through the next hour.

God always gives me just what I need when I need it. He gives me manna, not feasts, and it's perfect for me. It's enough to help me pause in the moment, whisper a prayer, and refocus on God.

Rachel—Short and Sweet

I've never been one to stick to doing long devotional plans. I will start them but rarely finish any. Instead, I like to find plans through my Bible app that are short and sweet—five days or fewer—so I can feel successful when I complete them. I'm always happy and feel better after I curl up on the couch with an afghan and a cup of coffee and spend time in the Word. It makes me feel like I made God smile, and I love reading familiar passages and noticing new details each time.

More often, though, I find myself talking to God throughout the day. It doesn't matter where I am or what I'm doing, I will visit with Him at random moments several times a day. He's always so available!

Jamila—Fasting for the Future

A few summers ago, I could feel God impressing upon my heart that I needed to start fasting. I had never done that before, so I had no idea what to think. All I knew was that if it was coming from the Lord, which I knew it was, then I needed to obey.

I didn't want my family to know what I was doing, so I planned to fast every weekday from seven in the morning until six at night. My lunch break would be my main time for more concentrated prayer, but it was an hour long. I had no idea how to pray for an entire hour! Thankfully, I found a plan on the YouVersion Bible app called The One Hour Prayer Cycle. It breaks the hour into twelve five-minute blocks of time centered around a different Bible verse for each cycle. It worked perfectly for me.

I used those lunch breaks to pray heavily for my family. I prayed that my kids would fall in love with Jesus. I prayed for my husband, that he would taste and see that the Lord is good, and that he would love his family as he should. I prayed for myself, that I would be the godly wife and mom I wanted to be.

Thirty days went by, and I still had no idea why I was fasting. I asked God, "Okay, do we stop now? Keep going? What's next?" About that time, I heard two different sermons on prayer. They both mentioned that sometimes we stop praying too soon. So, I kept going, still unsure why.

A few months later, I got my answer. Out of nowhere, I received a Facebook message from someone I didn't know informing me that my husband was having an affair. I knew then that the entire season of fasting had been preparing me to face what came next. I had grown closer to the Lord by leaps and bounds during that time. There's no way I could have gone through the end of my marriage, and maintained my integrity, without that time of spiritual growth.

But because of that season of fasting, I was able to wait on the Lord and rejoice in what He was doing in my life, even as I went through the divorce. I don't know what's going to happen next. But I do know that with God's help, I can choose my thoughts. I can praise God more than I complain. And I can continue being a blessing to my family, including my ex-husband.

I don't know why I've had to go through the things I've gone through—getting married late in life, losing a child, managing a blended family, divorce, and now single parenting. But maybe it has nothing to do with me at all. Maybe it's all so I can be a blessing to others.

Ashlee—Small Moments

As a mother of two girls under three with another child on the way, I find that my time is limited. Their naps don't often overlap, so I rarely get time by myself to be in the Word. Occasionally, I carve out moments when they're sleeping to pray through a psalm or study a book I'm working through, but most times, it's only two or three verses before my girls join me. I do what I can to focus my heart on the Lord throughout the day by having worship music playing in the background.

Thankfully, since my husband is a pastor, he has some flexibility in his schedule. On days when I'm really yearning for the Lord and needing to spend time alone with Him, my husband will come to relieve me for thirty minutes or an hour. These are the times when I can linger in God's Word.

I wish I could wake up an hour before my kiddos, but I'm so tired all the time it's just not feasible. I have to fight for my time in the Word every day. And every day looks different. If I don't get in the Word at all in a day, I try to sneak in praying through a psalm before bed, but even then, I usually doze off.

This season is busy, and finding time with God is a constant struggle. It makes those small moments I'm able to steep in Him that much more special.

Dee—Lifestyle over Routine

I keep a running prayer dialogue open all day. I don't have any close girlfriends to talk to, so Jesus is my go-to. I intentionally keep my eyes open for glimpses of Him throughout my day. A verse shared online. A butterfly in the garden. A caress of wind at just the right moment. I'm a homeschooling mom, so I get to delve into the Word with my kids studying memory verses, answering deep questions, or praying with them. It's an intentional all-day, everyday lifestyle, not just a routine sit-down-and-read-the-Bible-every-6-a.m. type of thing.

Guilt-Free Ideas for More

1. When you open your Bible, don't watch the clock.
2. Use an eye mask to help you block out distractions and focus as you listen to an audio Bible.
3. Develop the habit of talking to God throughout the day by setting a timer to beep at the top of every hour.
4. Talk to Jesus during commercials and ads.
5. Read Psalm 119 in one sitting.
6. Rather than one long quiet time, break your time with God into three smaller parts you can spread out between morning, noon, and night. For example, morning— prayer; noon—Bible reading; night—journaling.
7. Lay your Bible open on your kitchen counter. Every time you pass by, read a few verses.
8. Practice journaling your prayers with quick writes by setting a timer for three or five minutes. During that time, write as much as you can as fast as you can without worrying about spelling, handwriting, or complete sentences.
9. Light a scented candle or diffuse essential oils to engage your sense of smell as you read your Bible.
10. Incorporate movement into your time with God. Walk, stand, dance, pace, swim, stretch. Mow the lawn, do the dishes, sweep the floor.

Reflect and Discuss

1. Before this study, how long did you think your quiet time had to last? Where did that belief originate?
2. How has your opinion changed as a result of what you read?
3. How do you connect with God throughout the day?
4. What steps do you need to take to carve out time for a longer getaway with the Lord?
5. What simple, one-sentence prayers do you find yourself using again and again? What others could you add?

You Must Have Your Quiet Time Early in the Morning

Wake up! We are to honor God with our firstfruits, so if you do not have your quiet time first thing in the morning, you are essentially giving Him your leftovers. The proper quiet time involves getting up before everyone else in your household while it is still dark. It must still be dark because we are to be the light of the world, and light is more noticeable when it's dark. If you must have your quiet time at a different time of day because of your schedule or because you are not a morning person, it might be OK as long as you resign yourself to the fact that your days will not go as smoothly as they would have if you had started off on the right foot.

TRUTH: Dedicate each day to the Lord, then respond as He provides opportunities for connection with Him throughout the day.

Netflix and God

About the time I started teaching, I was also introduced to a deliciously bingeable show on Netflix. It was just the escapism I craved after long days of constant noise and stimulation. I'd crawl into bed each night, pull the covers to my chin, turn on my show . . . and promptly fall asleep.

Frustrated that I couldn't stay awake, and therefore never had any downtime, I started watching my show in the morning as I rushed through my half cup of coffee. My friends were right. The show was good. *Really* good.

I started waking up earlier.

Before long, my ten-minute morning Netflix date had stretched to an hour. Instead of dreading my alarm clock, I looked forward to hearing it. Instead of rolling out of bed each day, I popped up like a jack-in-the-box. The impossible had happened.

I had become a morning person.

I'd made it through birthing and nursing four humans without turning into one of "those" people. But somehow, several seasons of a random Netflix show that I can't even remember all these years later became my undoing.

When the show ended, I felt lost. *What do I watch now?* I thought, wandering in the glow of the moon each morning like a sad, lonely werewolf.

It was then, only after I'd spent several months unknowingly adjusting my biological clock, that I felt the gentle tap of the Lord. "You know," I sensed Him whispering to my soul, "since you're already awake . . ."

When Mornings Are Crazy and Chaotic

There's nothing that can divide a women's small group faster than morning versus evening quiet times. Oh, the friendships that have been ruined over this controversy!

Clearly, I've never been a morning-only quiet time person. When someone tells me they don't allow their feet to hit the floor without a proper time of reading the Bible and prayer, my first thought is, "Wow, thank you, Jesus, for this woman's amazing bladder!" I'm extra spiritual like that. My mind automatically goes straight to the practical side of this so-called rule.

When I was going through my seven- and- a- half years of birthing humans, it was biology, not my love for God, that woke me up every morning. I either had to eat, go to the bathroom, nurse a baby, or any combination of the three, and they all had to be done *now*. Had I tried to put off any of those things to read my Bible first, I would have only comprehended about one

one-hundredth of what I was reading, and I would have had more than one set of sheets to change. My quiet times would have had quantity but absolutely no quality.

Later, my mornings were filled with hungry children, a hyper dog, missing shoes, lunches that needed to be made, hair that begged to be combed, teeth that had to be brushed, and schedules that must be met. No matter how much I planned, no matter how much I prepared the night before, no matter how early I woke up, there was nothing calm, serene, or peaceful about the first two hours of the day.

That's not to say I never made a valiant effort to give morning quiet times a try. I did. But what happened more often than not was that two minutes after I settled in at the kitchen table with my Bible, I heard a cry from the crib or the pitter-patter of little feet rushing down the hall upstairs. Somehow my children's "mommy radar" could sense that I was awake early.

I became so frustrated that I began to resent the sound of my children's footsteps or my baby's cry, and by association, I was on the verge of resenting my children themselves. Didn't the kids know that morning was supposed to be the Lord's time? Didn't they know that mommy wasn't allowed to clock in until after Proverbs?

This left me stuck between my Bible and my breast pump with mommy duties on one side, quiet times on the other, lack of sleep under all of it, and a huge helping of guilt no matter which way I turned.

Maybe you've been there too. Maybe mornings are the most stressful time of your day. Maybe you can't think straight until you've had two cups of coffee. Maybe you're an on-call doctor or firefighter and must be out the door with only a few minutes' warning. Perhaps you're simply a dog mom, and it's your dog's tiny bladder, not your own, that rules your morning routine.

The point is not to have a contest to see whose mornings

are most chaotic. There's no stress level spectrum on which you must attain a certain level for God to grant you permission to opt out of morning quiet times. The point is simply to reassure ourselves that a crazy morning schedule is not an automatic sign that we're backslidden or faith failures.

The Power of a Morning Whisper

All that being said, we still can't ignore the innate power of a brand-new day. With morning comes a fresh start, a blank canvas, a ball of untapped potential. God incorporated expectation when He created the division of night and day. A new morning is like a gift of God's hope wrapped with rays of sunshine.

A recurring theme in the Bible gives weight to the importance of a brand-new morning. When the Israelites were in the desert, God provided manna for them every morning. For them, a new day was a new opportunity to depend on God.

When David kept his sheep in the pastures, he prayed to God early in the morning (see Psalm 5:3). For him, a new day was a new opportunity to praise God.

When the famous Old Testament warriors like Gideon and Joshua led their troops into battle, they often set out early in the morning. For them, a new day was a new opportunity to fight for God.

The morning holds promise. And it's hard to deny the benefits of starting the morning by reconnecting with God. But no matter how true this is, the existence of imperfect mornings is equally true.

For years, the combination of these two realities resulted in an overload of guilt. It wasn't until I experienced the power of a whisper that I fully found peace in the morning-only quiet time dilemma.

I finally realized that it didn't have to be all or nothing. Just because I couldn't drag out my study Bible, my concordance, my journal, and my highlighter every morning didn't mean I couldn't connect with God at all. I learned I could use one of my five-word prayers to dedicate the day to Him.

"Not my day, but yours." There's nothing magical or special about these specific five words. You can word your own whisper however you wish. The benefit is merely having something concise and simple that you can utter in a single breath.

When you pray, "Not my day, but yours," or anything similar, you acknowledge several things:

- Today is God's gift to you.
- How you live today is your gift to God.
- You're thankful and blessed because of today.
- You don't know what the day holds, but God does.
- No matter what the day holds, you will trust and rely on Him.

If you've struggled for years with not being able to manage a morning quiet time, create your own morning whisper. How can you dedicate each morning to the Lord in a simple but authentic way? How can you breathe a prayer of dependence, thanksgiving, and submission in just a sentence?

Save and guard your quiet time for later in the day when you're undistracted and able to give God your full attention. But as you open your eyes each morning, try letting Him know that you're thinking about Him with your first breath of the day.

Morning, Noon, and Night

The best time of day for you to spend dedicated time with the Lord is whenever it will work best for you. Perhaps it's when your kids and husband have gone off to school and work. Maybe it's fifteen minutes before you begin your workday. Maybe it's during your kids' nap time, or during lunch, or at the end of the day when your house is finally quiet.

David wrote in Psalm 55:17, "Evening, morning and noon I cry out in distress, and he hears my voice." There's no so-called right time of day to talk with God. He listens just as attentively in the evenings as He does in the mornings. Even Jesus communicated with God at night. He didn't force His life into a legalistic, morning-only ritual. Instead, He saw any time of day as a chance to meet with His Father.

I remember a time when my dad woke up at 2:00 a.m. every day to spend an hour in prayer and Scripture reading. When he was done, he'd go back to sleep until it was time for him to get up. For him, it worked. If I had tried to replicate his efforts, I would have fallen asleep with my cheek pressed flat up against 2 Chronicles. However, I've had seasons over the years when stress or sickness gave me chronic insomnia. In those instances, rather than fight the sleepless nights, I embraced them and relished the chance to enjoy God in the peace and quiet.

God does not keep office hours. He doesn't hang a sign on His door that reads, "Be back at 5:00 a.m." He doesn't give early bird specials to those who meet with Him before breakfast. He's a 24/7 God. Up all night. Up all day. Ready to meet with you whether the moon or the sun is lighting your way.

DEVOTIONAL MOMENTS FROM THE BIBLE

Midnight in the Garden with Jesus
Matthew 26:36–46; Mark 14:32–42; Luke 22:39–46

Above the tree canopy, as I imagine it, the moon's soft glow cast subtle shadows that shifted and danced as the wind blew through the olive trees. Only the strongest patches of moonlight sneaked past the branches and onto the paths below, settling like fog on the group of men I picture huddled together beside a tree trunk. Their eyes had grown so heavy that they barely noticed the moonlight or Jesus's voice riding the wind from a stone's throw away.

Jesus knew this garden and this particular grove of olive trees well. In His humanity, He had come here often to pray. In His divinity, His fingers had formed the very soil that now dirtied His knees. Tonight, in what He knew to be His most desperate hour yet, Jesus needed the familiar garden for a midnight moment with His Father.

The words came swiftly and easily. I imagine they'd been heavy on His heart since He'd ridden into Jerusalem earlier this week and had begun building like indigestion during the evening's Passover meal. Now, in the darkness, they were finally free to flow from Him unhindered and unrestrained.

He knew His Father was listening as surely as He knew that betrayal was, even now, on its way to the garden. He poured out His heart to His Father, pleading, begging, and submitting all in the same breath. I imagine the cool night air absorbing His sorrow and drying His face, perhaps muddied by a mixture of blood, sweat, and tears, as He prayed.

In between cries to His Father, He tried to wake His disciples, but it was no use. They did not yet understand. They had not yet come to appreciate the purity of prayers whispered in moonlight. But as He noticed the torchlight piercing through the night and invading the darkness of His garden from a distance, He knew that in time, they would.

Real Women, Real Stories

Peggy—A Song in the Night

I became a single mom of four when my husband left. Then my youngest daughter became increasingly difficult to manage when she was in elementary school. I consulted with doctors, but no one would help me. They insisted I was seeing things differently or misinterpreting symptoms because I was older now. But I knew they were wrong. I hadn't done anything differently with her than I did with the other three, but something was still off.

Finally, when she was in fourth grade, she was diagnosed with childhood-onset bipolar disorder and oppositional defiant disorder. A lot of my time with the Lord was spent driving in the car, trying not to cry. At night, after I read to the kids and put them to bed, I'd finally fall into bed myself, drained and exhausted.

I would try to read. Maybe pray. But most of the time, I'd whisper the lyrics of Twila Paris's song "The Warrior Is a Child" as I fell asleep. It talks about how a person can appear strong on the outside, but inside they're full of tears that only Jesus knows about. That was me. That song became my anthem.

I never gave up praying for my daughter and calling on God for help with her, and years later, I got to watch God answer those prayers. He touched her, saved her, and miraculously turned her life around. Now my children are grown and I'm retired, so I'm able to spend more time in my Bible than I could then. I do Precept inductive Bible studies regularly, and I mentor a younger mom at church. But a lot of my time with Jesus is still spent talking to Him about my daughter, trying to get a word from Him that I can pass on to her. Even when I am between Bible studies and don't do anything official for a quiet time, I'm still spending time with God. We just talk, you know? Sometimes it's as simple as that.

Christine—Conventional Routine

I follow a conventional routine for my quiet time. It's early in the morning, around 5:30, before everyone wakes up and before my workout. I sit in my kitchen or at my desk with a cup of coffee and a big glass of water. I have headphones to listen to the Bible and my physical Bible to read along while I listen. I use a notebook to take notes from a related podcast or to reflect on a daily devotion or a book I'm reading. Then I track my thoughts about Jesus and others in my prayer journal. The whole process takes about thirty minutes every day.

For me, the main thing is that I have to get it in before the house wakes. I'm a pastor's wife and homeschooling mom, so if I don't do it first thing in the morning, I won't get any more opportunities for quiet until bedtime.

Kim—Special Needs Child

I am a widow with an adult special needs child who lives at home with me. For years, Amy used to wake up at 4:00 a.m. all on her own, without an alarm. Now, thankfully, it's closer to 5:00 a.m. But when she wakes up, that's when she's the most talkative, and since I'm the only one around to listen, it's best to just let her talk.

Eventually we make breakfast and start a load of laundry or other household chores, but it's not until ten or later that I can even try to have a quiet time.

I have an area in my bedroom that has a table and a lamp, and it's a nice little setup. But when I try to go in there, or if I go into the office, Amy will forget what I'm doing, and she'll come find me pretty quickly. Even if I explain what I'm doing ahead of time, she just doesn't remember. She gets excited about things easily and wants to tell me right away.

But I've found that if I sit at the breakfast table with my Bible open and my study materials in front of me, because she can see me, it helps her remember that Mom is spending time with Jesus. She still interrupts, of course, but not as much.

The truth is, it's always a struggle, and there are times when nothing really works. Some seasons are just harder than others. Right now, my mom is in hospice, so I'm also dealing with her caregivers morning and night. Amy recently broke her foot. Then she started having GI issues. Last week we were at the doctor three times, and this week is going to be just as busy.

I never stop praying, of course, and I do apologize to God for not having a typical quiet time. But I say, "Lord, you know the situation," and I don't feel like He beats me up for it. You just have to do it when you can and keep up with the responsibilities that the Lord has placed in your lap.

Mary—Reciting Scripture

My husband has cancer, so I have many sleepless nights. I use this time to quote Bible verses I learned as a child. Psalm 23. Psalm 100. The Lord's Prayer. I say them over and over, along with many other passages. I also memorized the order of the New Testament books and came up with a method of how to remember them. For my daily Bible reading, I use an app that allows me to read the Bible through in chronological order. This is my second year using this program.

Jenna—Mom of Littles

My "quiet time" varies. I have four children under the age of five. I want them to see me reading my Bible, but I also know I can't dive deep with the constant interruptions. So I read things like Proverbs and the Psalms while they play, usually out loud so they hear it. I gave up the guilt of trying to wake up before my kids, so now, once everyone, including the baby, is asleep, I sit at my kitchen table and do my deeper Bible study.

Betsy—Just Plain Scripture

On a great day, my time with God will be in the afternoon when the boys and I are done with school for the day. But if things have been extra busy or if we've been out of the house, it might not happen until bedtime. No matter what, it won't be in the morning though because I am not a morning person.

It might look different from day-to-day, but most of the time I just read through the Scriptures. I use my physical Bible so I can write anything I want to remember about a passage in the margins and typically shy away from in-depth Bible study books because I've found that the questions distract me. Most of the time, I just want plain Scripture without the commentary. I might get stuck or get off track if I don't have a plan to stick to, but as long as I make a plan for myself, I can usually remain pretty consistent.

If I miss a day or two, I don't stress because I know that God isn't checking a box for me. But when I realize it's been several days or I'm suddenly out of the habit of quiet times, I know I need to reset. It's not that I feel guilty. It's that I feel that loss of connection that comes with spending time with the Lord.

Sharon—Early and Often

I like to get up early, before my husband, and read my Bible. Sometimes I read using a plan. Other times a certain Scripture will come to mind, so I'll look that up and end up reading that book of the Bible over several days. I try to read through the Bible at least every other year.

I pray during that time, but I also pray in the car, as I read prayer requests online during the day, and always when I look out my windows or walk outside. We live on a beautiful little lake in East Texas. You cannot look outside without thanking God and praising Him.

Guilt-Free Ideas for More

1. Write out a short prayer that you can whisper each morning.
2. Take a shower and use that time to talk to God. Thank Him for washing your sins away.
3. Go outside at night and read Psalm 8 while you stargaze.
4. Listen to a sermon during your morning or afternoon commute.
5. Keep a notebook on your nightstand and record five things you're thankful for before you go to sleep.
6. Schedule a lunch date with God. Imagine He is sitting beside you as you eat, and use that time to talk to Him.
7. Pick a time of day that corresponds to a family member's birthday. For example, 9:05 for September 5. Every time you look at a clock and see that time, pray for that person.
8. Subscribe to several email devotionals you can receive throughout the workday.
9. Set your alarm for 2:00 a.m. or 3:00 a.m. As the world around you slumbers, enjoy a middle-of-the-night conversation with God before going back to sleep.
10. Keep a Saturday morning clear on your calendar. Sleep in. Enjoy a slow, easy morning lingering in your Bible and enjoying the Lord's presence.

Reflect and Discuss

1. Describe the first two hours of your typical day.
2. Would you describe yourself as a morning person or a night person? Have you always been this way, or have you changed over time?
3. What time of day is it easiest for you to spend with God?
4. What time of day do you need Him the most?
5. What idea from this chapter are you most excited to try?

You Must Not Use Technology during Your Quiet Time

Log off! Technology is of the devil. Therefore, God cannot and will not use something so evil to communicate with you during your time with Him. You must use a black, leather-bound study Bible with footnotes and cross references printed so small they require a magnifying glass to read them. The inside cover must contain a family tree that goes back no fewer than ten generations, and the outside cover must be well-worn but not so tattered that it requires rebinding. Finally, the more the Bible weighs, the better.

TRUTH: The venue through which the Lord speaks is not nearly as important as your receptiveness and willingness to listen.

A Love Story

Days before we were to be married, my soon-to-be husband, Jason, stole my Bible.

It sounds rude and a bit scandalous, but the real issue is that I didn't even notice.

Swept up in last-minute wedding drama—which for us also included Christmas, a dog bite, a broken bone, and an awkward encounter with an ER doctor who just happened to be an ex-boyfriend with sudden power to decide whether hand surgery would require us to delay our honeymoon or not—it's safe to assume I didn't even pretend to read my Bible during the several days leading up to our big day.

It wasn't until our wedding night, when my new husband and I exchanged gifts, that I even realized my leather-bound *NIV Study Bible* by Zondervan had been missing. I opened the package Jason had so gingerly presented and wrinkled my brow. Why had Jason wrapped up a Bible that was already mine and given it to me in the first quiet moments of our new life together? I knew I had agreed to a modest lifestyle when I agreed to marry a minister, but this was a level of cheap even I had not anticipated.

That's when I noticed what was different. My new married name was now engraved in gold on the front cover.

I swooned.

He explained that he knew there would be endless places where I would have to change my name now that we were married, but by changing it on my Bible first, it would be a constant reminder that our marriage was a promise to God more so than a promise to each other.

I swooned again.

This Bible was the first Bible I read all the way through. My favorite verses were highlighted in sunshine yellow with notes, prayers, and thoughts scattered throughout the margins. It was already the most precious book I had ever owned, and now, with my new name and new meaning calling from the cover, it had become even more valuable.

I knew then that I would never read God's Word any other way.

Going Digital

And then we had kids.

It didn't take long for the promise I'd made with my physical Bible to become the first of many "nevers" I found myself retracting as the fantasies of motherhood gave way to reality.

My beautiful Bible was so big and heavy I couldn't manage it along with the kids, strollers, and diaper bags I had to juggle on Sunday mornings. I was like a really bad circus clown, dropping and chasing things a dozen times in as many steps, so I stopped bringing it to church. Then I became paranoid that one of my kids would rip its fine and delicate pages, so I stopped keeping it on my nightstand.

Though it felt at first like I was betraying a friend, I finally began exploring digital alternatives. Now, more than a decade later, almost all of my time with the Lord involves some form of technology. While my physical Bible will always hold a special place in my heart, I have been amazed by how much I've been blessed by digital resources.

But I've also been amazed by how much controversy this transition can stir up. Some wouldn't dream of sitting down with an iPad rather than a physical Bible to have a quiet time. Others turn up their noses at those in the congregation who pull out their smartphones during the sermon. It's as if they're constantly wondering if they're really on Facebook rather than the Bible app or if they're texting instead of taking notes.

Technology scares some people, and if you're someone who is reluctant to embrace it for your spiritual growth, your hesitations are justified. Without care, technology can lead to distractions, temptations, laziness, and waste. But with care, it can open doors to your spiritual growth that you never even realized were closed before.

The Evolution of Communication

The first thing to remember is that before computers changed how we read books, books changed how we read something else. Scrolls.

Anyone have a copy of the Bible written on a scroll? Why not? After all, that's what Jesus read from. He didn't have a handy pocket-sized Torah to pull out in the garden. He didn't have "Messiah" embossed on His leather-bound copy of the Psalms. Instead, He learned the Scriptures by hearing them and by reading from scrolls because that's how people communicated in His time.

The evolution of communication does not equate to the evolution of the Bible. Digital Bibles exist because how we communicate has changed, not because God's Word has changed.

We simply have the option of reading it on a screen now instead of rice paper, parchment, or papyrus.

When I first started really studying the Bible, I bought a huge, hardback dilapidated concordance in a library book sale for fifty cents. It was a great book because it smelled like a great book, with that musty attic aroma that tickles your nose and reminds you of your grandma.

Any time I wanted to dig deeper than the footnotes of my lime green Precious Moments Bible, I had to drag the concordance off the shelf, blow off the dust, and commit many minutes to flipping through the pages before finding an answer. The process was tedious, slow, and had significant limitations.

Now, it's a completely different story.

With just a few clicks, I have access to concordances, lexicons, sermons, translations, notes and outlines, and, in most cases, they all fit into my purse via my iPhone. If my son's cross country practice runs late, I can read a chapter or two from Ephesians in the pickup line at his school. If my daughter wants to look up a verse but we can't find her Bible, I can pull it up on my phone. If I've been meditating on a verse all day but want to look it up in a different version, I can do so at my computer.

Having my digital Bible at my fingertips has strengthened my communication with God because I always have whatever I need to have a quiet time.

My Digital Toolbox

Just a few minutes of searching online will show you that there are countless digital resources available to help you in your times with God. New sites and apps pop up daily. It would be impossible to give an exhaustive list of the pros and cons of everything that's available, but here are a few resources and features that have stood the test of time.

YouVersion Bible App

If I were stranded on a deserted technology island and could have only *one* app with me, my Bible app would be it. I use it several times a week, and it is by far my favorite spiritual growth tool.

My first choice is the YouVersion Bible app developed by Life.Church. It's a simple, free, digital Bible that is accessible on any device and available in hundreds of languages and translations. Someone installs the Bible app about once a second, and since its launch in 2008, it has been downloaded over five hundred million times!

After using the Bible app for many years, here are several things I love about it:

With the YouVersion Bible app, your Bible is always with you. Because of the offline accessibility, you have no excuse to put off reading. Your five minutes here or there can finally be used productively, and even if you can't have the full-blown quiet time you'd like, you can still spend time with God.

You can still take notes and highlight passages. It's built right into the functionality of the app, and you no longer have to worry about running out of room in the margins.

You can search the whole Bible at any time. If a friend frets about discovering her first (or hundredth) gray hair, but you've forgotten the verse that says "Gray hair is a crown of splendor," you can do a quick search in the app and find Proverbs 16:31 in less time than it takes to pluck a chin hair.

With so many translations at your fingertips, you can switch between versions in a snap! You no longer have to fret if your devotional book uses a different translation from yours. You can also *compare versions* with just a click, easily recognizing the subtle differences in word choices to gain deeper meaning of individual verses.

The Bible app has a built-in audio feature, so you can also listen to the Bible any time you want (in many versions). This means you can listen while driving to work, doing dishes, working in the garden, or running on your treadmill. (Pro tip: Whenever you come to a complicated word or name you have no idea how to pronounce, let the narrator do it for you!)

You can easily copy and share verses via social media, email, or text or use the Community feature and add friends to your network. What a way to encourage others as you spend time with the Lord.

It also has several different built-in reading and devotion plans for you to choose from. Options range from short, targeted plans you can complete in less than a week to yearlong plans to help guide you through the entire biblical narrative.

Going Deeper

When I want to dig even deeper into the Scriptures, I use other Bible study tools that are available digitally. Some of these academic resources used to be so expensive that only pastors and seminary students had access to them. Now, you can learn from some of the most well-respected theologians of our time without ever leaving your living room.

- Commentaries—explanations and interpretations of Scripture by various Bible scholars and theologians.
- Concordances—a list of words or phrases and where they occur elsewhere in the Bible. For example, with just a few clicks, you can find over two hundred verses that have the word *peace* in them.
- Encyclopedias—articles, outlines, and images to simplify the people, places, and terms of the Bible.

- Lexicons—definitions, pronunciations, and cross-references of words found in the original Old Testament Hebrew and New Testament Greek languages. For example, while English may translate a word to be *love*, the original language exposes the difference between *brotherly love* and *unconditional love*.

Getting Creative

Sometimes I want to play around during my quiet time. I want God to take me on an adventure! To transport me to another time. To unveil His deep, creative masterpiece and watch in wonder as the words pop off the page and perform for my soul.

Again, I could never capture an exhaustive list of tools He has used to help me explore during my time with Him, but here are a few of my unconventional favorites:

Digital Notetaking. Last summer, I bought my first iPad so I could try taking notes digitally. Writing things down helps me process them. I literally think with my hands. What I found was that writing digitally not only preserved the power of handwriting for me, but it also helped tamper my perfectionist tendencies. I now take all my sermon notes on my iPad and use it several times a week for writing out my prayers.

Map. For some odd reason, the Maps section of physical Bibles is usually the first thing to fall out when the binding gets weak. Now, with just a few quick keystrokes, you can see for yourself just how far the Israelites had to march around the walls of Jericho or what modern-day country is in the place of ancient Babylon.

Music. Entire playlists are now available for almost any mood you could imagine. If you want to praise God as you clean your house, go for it! If God used a song to speak to your heart on Sunday, you can replay it during your time with Him on Monday. If you want instrumental hymns playing softly in the background to help you focus during your time with the Lord, nothing is holding you back.

Podcasts. Listen to your favorite preachers from around the world whenever it's convenient for you. Discover true stories and interviews with real people living out God's call on their lives. Use podcasts like *The Bible Recap* to help you understand God's Word as you read through it. The possibilities are so endless, the greatest problem is running out of time.

Scripture Memory. Did you know that they now have apps specifically for memorizing Scripture? Several are available, so as you search for one that will work for your goals, consider price (not all are free), translations (some offer only one or two translations), and whether or not you can import your own verses. Feel free to keep it simple and just use your "Notes" app (or something similar) as an avenue to review Bible verses, and don't forget to explore general applications for memorization such as digital flashcards as well.

Timelines. Search "interactive Bible timeline" to discover one of my favorite free tools. You can not only wrap your head around the order of historical events in the Bible, but also click the live links to learn more about each event.

Videos. If you've never been to Israel, it might be hard to imagine the terrain, vegetation, and geography of the Holy Land as you read God's Word. Thankfully, you can search for just about any biblical site and get a video commentary to see it for yourself. Another more specific video resource I can't recommend highly enough is The Bible Project. This ministry takes big concepts and topics in the Bible and creates simple, beautifully animated videos to explain them. The animation and narration are artistic and professional, and all of their videos are free.

Turning It Off

Technology can be your best friend or your worst enemy. Don't get weighed down by someone else's digital toolbox if it's more frustrating than helpful. If you want, you could use technology for every aspect of your quiet time, from setting an alarm as a reminder to read your Bible to journaling to tracking your prayer requests to composing original praise music.

Or, if the thought of mixing technology with your quiet time makes you more uncomfortable than a Baptist buying cooking wine, you could simply turn everything to *off* and use technology that way too.

Moses and a Message

Exodus 24:15–18; 31:18

Two months after the Israelites fled from Egypt, their journey of escape brought them to the base of Mount Sinai. As they set up camp, the Lord called Moses to meet with Him on the mountain so He could confirm His covenant with Israel.

As Moses began one of his many ascents up the rocky terrain, the glory of the Lord settled on the mountain in the form of a cloud. To the Israelites, it looked like a fire burning from the mountain's peak. To Moses, it likely mirrored the familiar flames of the burning bush.

For forty days, he remained on the mountain with the Lord, praying, fasting, listening, and recording God's commands for His people (Deuteronomy 9:9). Finally, when the Lord finished speaking, Moses watched as God chose ten of those commands as a paragon above all the others, inscribing each one himself onto two stone tablets for Moses to bring to His people.

To read about it now, thousands of years later, the moment seems primitive and archaic. How cumbersome to engrave text letter by letter. What an inconvenience to travel with the burden of stone tablets weighing you down. But the Israelites didn't see it as a burden at all. Instead, they saw the miraculous word from God for what it was. A treasure. A prized possession to be protected, guarded, and honored as holy.

If you consult the armchair theologians of the internet today, you'll find this exchange memorialized on T-shirts, coffee mugs, and memes as the humorous origins of technology in the Bible. Moses, as they say, was technically the first man to download data from the cloud onto a tablet.

What God's people once carried in a sacred chest of acacia wood and gold, we now carry in our pockets and purses. But while, with new methods of delivery, the weight of the words has lightened, the true *weight* of the words has not. From stone tablet to computer tablet, God's Word remains forever.

Real Women, Real Stories

Teri—All Digital

My quiet time is all over the place. I try to do it in the mornings, but because of my work schedule, that doesn't always happen. During busy seasons, I travel almost every week, so I keep everything on my phone. I suppose I could carry around my Bible and books and pull everything out when I need it, but for me it's so much easier to be 100 percent digital. My phone is light and compact and easy to access. Since it's with me all the time anyway, I might as well use it for my relationship with God.

For years I've used the devotional and reading plan from Our Daily Bread as a guide to read through the Bible in a year, and now it's available in an app as well. I can access it no matter where I am, and it easily links me to BibleGateway where I can read, highlight, and take notes anytime I want. I like that I can listen to someone else read the Bible for me because I focus better if I can hear it and read it at the same time.

The best part is that when I'm sitting at an airport waiting for a flight and realize I haven't done my Bible study yet, I can just put in my earbuds and, in the middle of all the chaos, I can talk to God.

Shelly—Slow and Steady

For the past two years I've been studying my way through the Bible at a snail's pace. I use the Proverbs 31 First 5 app for my independent study and absolutely love it! [Developed by Proverbs 31 Ministries, the First 5 app offers daily devotions and teachings from God's Word.] I can go at my own speed and not have to rush to meet a deadline someone else has imposed on me.

I usually sit in my dining room that has become more of a sitting room. As long as I get up early enough, it's a great place for me to "get alone with God." If not, then our dogs insist on sharing my space with me, sometimes, even in my lap, and other family members wander in as well. My daughter will want to play the piano or pet the dogs. My husband will come to look out the front windows or talk about something on his mind. If I want to have that uninterrupted time with God, I have to do it in the early morning hours.

Neisha—Coffee and Jesus

Simply stated, my quiet time consists of coffee and Jesus. But, of course, it's a little more complicated than that.

Over the years, I struggled with making time for Bible reading unless I was held accountable within a study group, or I looked at it as a checklist item I *had* to complete to be worthy. Life is *messy*, and any time devoted to self-care felt selfish in comparison to caring for my children, my husband, the house, or health issues.

On top of that, I couldn't manage to find the right time of day to have my quiet time. Because of my night-owl personality, morning quiet times were unappealing. Daytime devotionals were hard to manage with a growing family of challenging children. And nighttime devotionals always seemed "too little, too late" or disrespectful to my husband who waited all day to spend time with me.

Because of this, I began praying for God to wake me up early with an insatiable appetite for His Word. I couldn't squeeze in focused time with my Bible in my bustling house without some kind of divine help. In time, He answered my prayers abundantly!

Now, I wake before my children, grab a cup of coffee, and sit down for Bible study at my desk almost every morning. I found that my ADHD [attention deficit hyperactivity disorder] mind cannot be engaged with lightweight, quick devotionals. They tend to make my mind wander. Instead, I have to do deeper, expository studies of books of the Bible to engage my brain and keep my mind focused.

I have found resources like First 5 study guides offer a simple, uncomplicated guide through books of the Bible so God can show me how seemingly unrelated texts can completely apply to my life situations. I also enjoy inductive Bible studies that drive my mind into the depths of Scripture and remind me of the correlations between passages all across the Bible. I have also learned to use the Blue Letter Bible app to look up the original language on both unfamiliar and overfamiliar words to help me see the true, deeper meaning of the original text that English may have diluted.

Using a journaling Bible and annotating with colorful pens

help my visual mind remember nuggets of truth much better. Whenever I buy a new Bible to replace my tattered one, I use my morning quiet times to go book by book and transfer these notes from my old Bible to my new one. It gives me a chance to revisit all the beauty and truth God has revealed over the years, and it drives His Word deeper into my memory. I am able to see how Bible stories connect between books and on the greater timeline of history, and it always reveals wisdom for my immediate needs.

My physical Bible has become my companion. I recognize the words it contains are not just published literature but the very words of God! And He is waiting to use them in a conversation with me *all the time*! I determine whether that conversation gets started by whether or not I show up, and when I do show up, it results in intimacy with Jesus! This intimacy blesses my other relationships, gives me wisdom in parenting, and helps me live in a state of peace within chaos. My priorities fall into line, and even my kids notice a difference in me. They realize that the combination of coffee and Jesus isn't just my routine or a favorite thing, but it is the most necessary and important part of my life. It makes me the loving mom they want to have around.

Helen—My God and My iPad

I started having regular quiet times with the Lord during my husband's last years of fighting cancer. I would use my iPad to search the Bible so I wouldn't have to turn on the light and disturb him. I spent many hours just sitting close to him or waiting at the hospital. Often times, something would happen that would cause me to seek or praise God. It could be as simple as waking up to a beautiful day, seeing a cloud, feeling a gentle breeze, or noticing a squirrel. God would bring a thought to mind, and I would write it in my iPad. Other times, I would study my Sunday school lessons or rewatch church services. If I was by myself,

I'd sing Christian songs and hymns, but if not, I would still sing, though silently.

Now, I still use my iPad all the time to read and search the Holy Bible for whatever I need to learn that day. I always have it close by so I can write whatever God tells me. My quiet time is usually before I go to bed and right before I get up. I am so thankful to God for patiently waiting for me to grow and learn about His love for me.

Guilt-Free Ideas for More

1. Go to biblegateway.com or bible.com, and read Psalm 23 in four different translations: New International Version, New Living Translation, King James Version, and *The Message*.

2. Look at photos of outer space taken from the James Webb Space Telescope at webb.nasa.gov, and praise God for creating the amazing universe. Write down five words that describe how big God is.

3. Look at photos taken of microscopic objects in Nikon Small World Photomicrography Competition at nikonsmallworld.com, and praise God for His amazing attention to detail. Write down five small details that you're trusting God for right now.

4. Watch Carrie Underwood and Vince Gill sing "How Great Thou Art" on YouTube.

5. Ask a trusted friend or mentor to recommend a podcast for spiritual growth.

6. Visit futureme.org, and write an email to your future self. What is God teaching you that you may forget later? Record those lessons now, and choose to remember them in a month, a year, or on any random day in the future.

7. Watch the live stream of your church's Sunday morning service and actively worship in your living room.

8. Take a social media fast for a predetermined length of time. Use that time instead to deepen your relationship with God.

9. Explore resources offered through The Bible Project at bibleproject.com. Choose several videos to incorporate into your time studying God's Word.

10. Use the Notes feature on your phone to record prayer requests.

Reflect and Discuss

1. Does technology inspire you or scare you? Why?
2. How much time do you think you typically spend each week on social media? Streaming services? Texting? If you can, check your screen time and see if your estimates are correct.
3. What quiet time tools are already in your digital toolbox?
4. What tech tool do you think might help you most in spending time with God?
5. How might you benefit from a break from technology?

You Must Have Your Quiet Time Every Single Day

Don't skip! God does not take vacation days, and neither should you. If you do skip a day, consider that a completely wasted day. God was not in it at all. In order to get back on track, you must double up on your quiet time the following day, spending extra time confessing your sins, of course. Consider each day you skip as taking one step farther away from God. It will take at least that number of days of consistent quiet times in order for you to be close to Him once again. Therefore, if you skip a whole month, it will take a whole month to get back on track.

TRUTH: Your goal of spending time with the Lord should be consistency and constant connectedness to Him, not perfection.

If You Really Love God

It took hours of strategic planning, NATO-style negotiations, and a surplus of goldfish crackers, but the moment had come at last—all four tiny humans were preoccupied, safe, and content. The newborn slept soundly in his floor bassinet. The middles were caught up in an animated world glowing from the television like an alien mothership. And the six-year-old stabbed tiny toothpicks into Play-Doh at the kitchen table.

My time had come at last.

Quietly and carefully, I maneuvered off the couch and shuffled down the hallway in my socks. My insides sloshed and jiggled, still trying to settle back into place after my fourth C-section. I wrapped myself in a bear hug until I made it to the bathroom where I slid inside and locked the door.

What a sweet sound—that lock. It was the sound of solitude. Of peace. The sound of sweet relief, praise Jesus!

At the risk of oversharing, let me remind you what happens during a C-section. After being prepped by a team of nurses, you're visited by a messenger from the Lord called an anesthesiologist. He or she dispenses a miracle drug into your rounded back, and in seconds, every body part from your rib cage down Rip van Winkles into a deep, deep slumber.

Waking up your body after the first C-section is like waking a child for school after spring break. It takes a little extra coaxing and shaking, but eventually she rolls out of bed, annoyed but accepting that the break wasn't longer.

But waking up your body after a fourth C-section is like trying to wake up a teenager after an entire summer of sleeping in. It takes patience, persistence, and sometimes, divine intervention. And the most stubborn of all body parts, and therefore the last to awaken, is always your bowels.

Just seconds after I locked the door and settled into place to finally take care of my most basic of bodily functions, the noises began. A thump. A cry. Another cry. A scream. "Mooommmmy!" Footsteps. Then knocking which morphed to pounding on the bathroom door.

They found me.

As I rose and dressed again, frustrated, dejected, and still in pain, I heard one last noise. It wasn't the still, small voice of the Lord. No, this one had a bit of an edge to it.

"If you really love God," it hissed in my ear, "you'd find a way to have perfect quiet time right now."

When Life Gets in the Way

Oh, how I wish I could go back in time to my younger self, take her swollen hands in mine, and whisper the truth I never heard back then.

Even Jesus missed a quiet time.

We don't hear that sermon on Sunday mornings, do we? But, rest assured, frazzled friend, it happened. And if it happened to Him, it's going to happen to us.

No doubt you've experienced similar seasons of chaos in your own life. Times when your own needs were eclipsed by the needs of others. Times when you couldn't even poop in private, much less pray. Maybe your husband was deployed for a year. Maybe you had to spend months cleaning out your childhood home after your parents passed away. Maybe you were grading term papers, meeting a deadline, grieving, moving, traveling, or hosting overnight guests.

And in the middle of the chaos, a voice in the back of your mind created a constant, white noise of guilt that you couldn't seem to escape: "If you really loved God, you'd find a way. If you were holier, you'd make it happen. If God is really your top priority, you'd never miss a quiet time at all."

When Responsibility Trumps Intention

In Matthew 14, Jesus experienced quiet-time frustrations as well. The Bible is clear that He withdrew often to pray, and on this particular day, His desire to spend time with His Father was extremely great. He had just learned that His relative and friend, John the Baptist, had been beheaded by King Herod.

Imagine how He felt when He heard that news. Imagine how His heart hurt and how much He wanted to seek God and be comforted by the Holy Spirit in that moment. So He did what was natural for Him: "He withdrew by boat privately to a solitary place" (Matthew 14:13). He tried to get away, and He tried to get alone. Two objectives for having a perfect quiet time.

But that's where it stopped, with a boat full of good intentions. "Hearing of this, the crowds followed him on foot from the towns" (v. 13). He tried to get away. But the people followed Him, found Him, and interrupted His time with His Father before it even began.

Sound familiar?

In these situations, when our intentions are interrupted by our responsibilities, it's easy to get frustrated. When you finally manage to wake up before your family only to hear footsteps in the hall two seconds after you open your Bible, it's easy to resent the person responsible for the footsteps. When you choose to have your quiet time during your lunch break, it's easy to become irritated when your boss or work bestie stops by to chat.

"Why won't everyone just leave me alone?!" you think, and close your Bible with another pound of guilt weighing you down.

If Jesus reacted like we do, we'd expect Him to feel extreme dread and resentment when He arrived on land and to chastise the crowd for following Him on foot. After all, they were keeping Him from being able to do the holy and right thing—have a perfect quiet time.

But Jesus didn't scold the people who needed Him. Instead, "When Jesus landed and saw a large crowd, he had compassion on them and healed their sick" (v. 14). He didn't scold them. He healed them. He didn't ignore them. He loved them. And He didn't turn them away so He could feed himself spiritually. Jesus drew them closer so *He* could feed *them*—spiritually and physically.

As Soon as Possible

It's important, however, that we not ignore the rest of this story. It's not enough just to embrace our responsibilities and blessings even when they interfere with our quiet times. It's equally important to follow through on our original intentions, just like Jesus did.

If we're not careful, our days of missed quiet times will turn into weeks, weeks will turn into months, and before long, our seasons of chaos will turn into a lifetime of excuses.

But that won't happen if we do what Jesus did. He got back to His quiet time as soon as possible.

After He was interrupted by the crowd, He spent a whole day caring for them. He ended the evening by taking five loaves of bread and two fish and feeding the entire crowd of more than five thousand people. But as soon as everyone's needs were met and the people left, "He went up on a mountainside by himself to pray" (v. 23).

Jesus may have missed the quiet time He intended to have earlier in the day, but even while He was distracted by a tangent of obligations, He never forgot where His heart was headed. He remained focused on His Father, and when the first window of opportunity opened for Him to return to His original plan for solitude and prayer, He took it.

A Different Walk in Different Seasons

Because your relationship with God will always be affected by ever-changing variables and seasons of life just like other relationships, it's natural for it to change and evolve over time. It's not a robotic, linear progression that advances like soldiers marching in a parade. Instead, it's an organic connection that responds and behaves more like soldiers on a battlefield. It's real. It's unpredictable. It's dodging bullets and grenades of sick children, traffic jams, electric bills, house guests, final exams, funerals, and a million other demands that fight to bring it down.

There will be seasons of your life when you can spend hours

of uninterrupted time poring over your Bible, praying the stars down from heaven, and journaling daily manifestos for Jesus. When you're in those seasons, soak it up! Enjoy them! Take every last advantage of the time you have with God and don't waste those years on mindless entertainment or disposable relationships.

Because there will also be seasons of your life when you have to fight for every single minute you spend with God. The time may come when you can't even find your Bible much less five uninterrupted minutes to sit alone reading it. In those seasons, you have three choices:

1. Guilt—Ride the wave of guilt as you keep trying and failing to keep your quiet times unaffected by your lifestyle changes.
2. Goodbye—Since you feel it's got to be all or nothing, and it clearly can't be all, throw in the towel and say goodbye to all attempts at time with Jesus until the chaos subsides.
3. Grace—Understand that you have more to balance now, and adjust accordingly. You might not be able to spend an entire hour a day reading your Bible. Some days, you may be doing well just to read one verse. You may spend less time journaling and more time meditating. Or you may pray more often with your eyes open than you do with your eyes closed. Adopt Jesus's example of handling your responsibilities without resentment or guilt, but be proactive in responding to the first available opportunities to pray and seek solitude.

The more your time with God can bend and flex, the less likely it is to break apart.

Alternatives to Daily Quiet Times

If you've been swimming in guilt because you've never been able to master the everyday, without fail, quiet-time goal, perhaps you could adjust your goals to fit within a weekly schedule instead of a daily one. I'll never forget the first time I heard of this option. I was talking to a friend who worked as a nurse in a busy emergency room. Her job consisted of four twelve-hour days most weeks. On the days that she worked, she barely had time to commute to the hospital, work her shift, eat, and sleep, let alone spend thirty minutes in perfect, pretty quiet time with the Lord.

When I asked her how in the world she found time to study the Bible when so many of her hours were already spoken for each day, she simply brushed it off. She said she did all of her Bible study on her off days and made sure she spent quality time each week with the Lord rather than try to go through the motions on a daily basis.

Until then, I had never considered that possibility. But the more I thought about it, the more logical it seemed. And the more it seemed to mirror a true relationship rather than a meaningless ritual.

There is also another thing that can help during those times when the demands of life have caused you to drift further and further away from the intimate relationship with the Lord that you desire: a long getaway. It may come in the form of an annual women's retreat or a church conference or just an afternoon escape once a month. You may travel to the mountains, or you may travel to Starbucks. The details are not as important as fulfilling the need to get away with God.

If you're married, you may have experienced the benefits of going on a kid-free vacation with your husband. If you're single, you have probably cherished the trips you've taken with your girlfriends. There's just something about spending an extended period of uninterrupted time with those you love. It breathes life back into your relationships. It reminds you why you care about them. It gives you the ability to go back and face the everyday challenges with a little more strength and clarity.

Your relationship with the Lord will benefit from a getaway even more.

Embrace your responsibilities as blessings, not burdens. Consider your time with God a privilege, not an obligation. Fuel your relationship with grace, not guilt.

Run away with Him, as much and as often as you are practically able, and see how you return changed.

DEVOTIONAL MOMENTS FROM THE BIBLE

Peter's Erratic Beginning
Matthew 16:13–23

No one modeled the never-ending struggle for consistent time with the Lord more than Peter. In Matthew 16, Peter had the New Testament equivalent of a perfect quiet time. It started when Jesus was talking to His disciples and asked them point blank, "Who do you say I am?" (v. 15).

Peter answered, "You are the Messiah, the Son of the living God" (v. 16).

In case you're keeping score, in the world of perfect answers, that was pretty much the most perfect, most accurate, best answer ever. It was spot-on and revealed the purity and courage in Peter's heart. He recognized who Jesus was and declared it without shame. Peter's answer blessed Jesus, and Jesus's reply charged Peter with the

Guilt-Free Quiet Times

honor of being a pillar of the New Testament church. "You are Peter, and on this rock I will build my church" (v. 18).

What an amazing moment. A face-to-face with Jesus that starts with the perfect question, is followed by the perfect answer revealed to Peter by God the Father (v. 17), and ends with the perfect application. It's the formula for a perfect quiet time if there ever was one.

But just four verses after Jesus's response—not forty, not four hundred, just four teeny verses later—Peter messes up big time. He rebukes Jesus and tells Him that He doesn't have to be killed and raised on the third day. "Never, Lord!" Peter says. "This shall never happen to you!" (v. 22).

Jesus's reply isn't as sweet this time. In fact, it's downright harsh. Jesus turns and says to Peter, "Get behind me, Satan! You are a stumbling block to me; you do not have in mind the concerns of God, but merely human concerns" (v. 23).

Don't you just love it when you act like Satan just two seconds after talking with God? Good times.

But the hope lies in that Peter got a second chance. In fact, he had chance after chance after chance, and no matter how much Peter messed up, Jesus never gave up on him.

Peter walked on water, but then he sank. He prayed with Jesus, but then he fell asleep. He stuck with Jesus, then he denied Him three times. He messed up time and time again, but with every screw up, he grew up. He grew closer to the Lord, stronger in his faith, and bolder in his ability to act out his faith.

And so can you.

Real Women, Real Stories

Allison—Permission Granted

I went through a huge chunk of my life with a lot of guilt either because I was not having a quiet time every day or because I was, but to be completely honest, I wasn't enjoying it much. My time with God felt very much like an obligation.

It wasn't until a few years ago that I finally realized this idea was not working. Either I needed to get my heart right with God, or I had to figure out something else because I couldn't handle the guilt anymore. If this was what God wanted from me, He was going to have to give me joy in doing it.

I took my time praying about it, talking to a few people I trusted, and researching on my own, and I realized that somewhere along the way, I had confused *abiding* in God with opening my Bible and reading something every day. Those are *not* the same thing. I was doggedly going through the motions of having a "proper" daily quiet time and was wearing myself out because that's what I thought I had to do. The only way for me to shift my focus and push past that pattern of guilt was to give myself permission not to open my Bible every day.

Everything changed once I gave myself that break. I began to feel the Holy Spirit drawing me gently to the Lord rather than guilt shoving me to Him. It stopped being a checklist. It stopped feeling like spiritual drudgery. Instead, my time with the Lord became sweeter. More intimate. Now I may not read my Bible every day, but I do read it consistently, and that has been world-changing for me.

Since then, I've never gone four days without opening my Bible. It's usually every other day or, to my surprise, every day, and I find myself spending more time with Him than I ever did before. Each time I open my Bible, I am aware of how much

I miss it, and my quiet time is now one of my favorite parts of my day.

It's like when you put a child down for a nap. You're so excited to get him down and then two hours later you're wishing he was awake again. You've missed him because you had a chance to miss him.

I think that's how my quiet time changed. It's like my soul finally had a chance to long for the Lord.

Angie—Bible Study versus Devotions

For my quiet times, I prefer using devotional books that are usually laid out according to the date. Sometimes I read on my own; other times I read with my girls. As they've gotten older, it's gotten harder and harder to find time when all three are home at once, so we take advantage of any time we can. Sometimes we'll even take turns reading in the car—one devotion on the way out, another on the way home.

I also do regular homework-style Bible studies when they're offered through my church. But even when I'm studying the Bible for a class, I don't really count that as my devotional time. I see that as investing in what I'll need for the future, but my devotional time gives me what I need for today.

Meghan—Tea and Consistency

I've always struggled with consistency during my quiet times. I'll be really good about sticking with it for a few weeks, and then I get distracted by the busyness of life and slack off. So, over the years, I've tried to come up with different ways to make my quiet times more of a one-on-one time with God as opposed to a daily duty I'm required to fulfill.

When my daughters were young, I would have my quiet time in the afternoon when I was sitting in line waiting to pick them up from school. This was the only time of day when I wouldn't be distracted by things I could be doing at home, so it was the best fit for me. I would deliberately arrive to school thirty minutes early so I could spend that time with God.

Another approach I use is my "tea time/quiet time." I have a really yummy spiced tea that I only drink while I'm having my quiet time. I really like this tea (a little too much, honestly), so this helps me look forward to having my quiet time. It's the same way I feel when I plan to meet my friends at a local café and chat over brunch. I find myself looking forward to my tea time with God when He and I can chat and spend that intimate time together over a cup of spiced tea.

Karen—Habit Stacking

I've found it helpful to stack habits of intimacy with Jesus on top of something I'm already doing in my daily schedule. For example, when I go for a morning walk on the beach, I stick my prayer cards in my pocket and put some instrumental worship music in my earbuds. When I reach the end of the beach, I sit on an old, weathered log and pray looking out at the ocean. Prayer cards are my way of staying focused and not drifting off into other thoughts when I'm praying. I have one person or prayer point per card, and I shuffle through them, praying out loud.

My second daily habit is to make a cup of coffee after lunch and read my Bible. I underline and mark up passages as I read because it helps me stay focused.

Using those two routines in my day to meet with Jesus means I'm far less likely to forget my quiet times. Going for a walk and having a coffee are two habits I rarely, if ever, miss. They are milestones in my day that I look forward to.

I also really like splitting my quiet time into two parts so I can devote all my attention to either prayer or Bible reading, without feeling rushed. I like to dive deep and linger in God's presence, so this pattern gives me the opportunity to do so even on busy days. And if some days things go pear-shaped for whatever reason, I have another opportunity already built into my day to grab hold of that time with Jesus.

Guilt-Free Ideas for More

1. Choose a task that you do regularly, such as taking a shower, waiting in line, or cooking dinner, and use that time to pray.

2. Have a day of thanksgiving, not in November, during which you thank God for every blessing that you can think of throughout your day.

3. Use Sunday as a genuine day of Sabbath rest. Take a nap. Take a walk outside. Recharge your soul by reflecting on God's goodness.

4. Go on a mission trip, if you are able. If you are not, partner with a missionary from your church by praying daily for his or her trip.

5. Choose one chapter of the Bible, and read it five times in one week.

6. At the beginning of the year, before any other conflicts arise, schedule one or two vacation days from work that you can set aside entirely for God. Use that time as He guides you.

7. On the first of each month, have a "meeting" with God. Reflect on the prior month, and ask Him to guide your plans, goals, and calendar for the month ahead. Use Jeremiah 29:11–13 as the framework for this time.

8. Take a purposeful short break from your Bible. Allow yourself time to hunger for God's Word. When you return, feast on His truth with fresh longing and appreciation.

9. Observe Advent in June when you are not caught up in the usual Christmas chaos of buying gifts, decorating, and attending parties. Reflect on the birth of Jesus. Sing Christmas hymns. Anticipate His second coming.

10. Memorize one verse of the Bible each week for a year.

Reflect and Discuss

1. Does your schedule typically vary from day-to-day, or does it stay the same?
2. Describe a season of your life when you had the most discretionary time. What did your quiet times look like then?
3. When have you felt resentful for having to manage interruptions to your normal routine?
4. When you're in a season of life where it's difficult to spend time with God on a daily basis, how do you usually react? By feeling guilty? By saying goodbye to quiet times until life gets easier? Or by accepting God's grace and adjusting your expectations?
5. Describe a time when you've been able to escape with God for an afternoon, an evening, or even a weekend.

Myth 6

You Must Journal during Your Quiet Time

Write it out! The unwritten eleventh commandment is "thou shalt journal," so if you're not journaling during your quiet time, expect serious consequences like fire, brimstone, boils, or at the very least, car trouble. Journaling is the magic step of your quiet time in which insight turns to application and God applauds your brilliance. Proper journaling is handwritten with a fountain pen into a hardback Moleskine notebook. Printing is acceptable. Cursive is better. Calligraphy, of course, is best. Finally, if you don't post a pic and tag it with #biblejournaling, #amjournaling, and #ilovejesus, you might as well burn the whole thing in a bonfire.

TRUTH: Your time with the Lord should result in a life well lived, not just a life well documented. Respond to Him however the Holy Spirit prompts you.

Can You Help Me?

I tiptoed into the small prayer room at church, grateful for the extra time before service, and sighed with contentment to find I was alone. *Wait, I shouldn't be happy about an* empty *prayer room*, I realized, and quickly sidestepped into repentance as I settled on the front pew.

Still, it was nice to think and meditate in solitude for a change, and it wasn't long before I was opening my iPad to write out my prayer in my digital journal. "Dear God," I began, because my written prayers are always way more formal than my unwritten ones. "Can you help me?"

I paused and thought about that one simple request. Of

course, God *can* help me. Perhaps that was the wrong word. I deleted the question and began again. "Will you help me?"

Better. Closer. But something still felt off. I deleted and tried once more. "I know you'll help me. Thank you in advance for carrying me through this."

There. That's what I really wanted to say. Now my words really reflected my faith.

I should share this online, I thought.

Before the thought had a chance to land in my head, I was screen recording, editing, posting, tagging, and commenting to my heart's delight, careful to get everything just right so as to encourage the largest number of virtual Jesus-seekers possible.

Just as I was feeling #blessed about encouraging others from the comfort of the prayer room at church, it hit me. I was in the *prayer* room and hadn't even gotten around to praying.

Oops. Perhaps I needed more help than I realized.

If You're Not a Writer

Social media has taken journaling to a whole new level. It's no longer a world of dear-diary moments captured in spiral-bound notebooks from the grocery store. Now it's doodles and stickers and templates and markers and online courses on how to perfectly hand letter properly, so every written word can look extra scrolly and holy.

But what if your handwriting is sloppy? What if you have dyslexia or dysgraphia? What if your spelling is ~~atroshush~~ atrocious?

Or worse yet, what if you don't even like writing?

Good news, friend. Jesus wasn't a writer either. Not that we know of anyway. All we know is that not one word of the entire Bible was written by Him.

Now, hold your white horses. I know the entire Bible was

written by God, and Jesus is God in the flesh, so technically, He wrote the whole thing. But you know what I mean.

Jesus taught. He served. He healed and performed miracles and poured His life into people.

But He didn't write.

So if you're not a writer either, there is no reason for you to feel obligated to respond to God by journaling.

The point of journaling is to process your thoughts so they translate into actions. When people journal, they may record Bible verses that speak to them, prayer requests that burden their hearts, sins about which they feel convicted, or a dozen other things.

But journaling is only a means to an end.

The goal is to live our lives in such a way that our actions reflect our time with the Lord. If the only way for others to see that you've spent time in God's Word is by seeing how many journals you have on your shelf or how artistic your doodles are in the margins of your Bible, then your time has not been productive.

Others should be able to see Christ in you by how you live, not by how you write about it.

How to Journal, If You Want To

That's not to say that there aren't valid benefits to journaling. Many say it helps clear away the mental clutter and reduce stress and anxiety. Others claim it helps diffuse anger, cope with depression, or process complicated feelings.

So if you'd like to explore journaling, but just aren't quite sure how to do it, you'll be happy to know that there is no right way to journal.

Writing in a journal is very personal. Some people, like me, can focus on prayer more easily if they write out their prayers to God. That's one form of journaling. Others write Bible verses in their own words so that they can understand them more easily. That's another way. Others may write out what they plan to do differently as a result of a particular passage they read.

All of those are examples of how to journal, but they are not requirements. You need only to look to the Bible to see that any kind of writing is acceptable. Paul wrote letters. David wrote songs. Moses captured history. John recorded his dreams.

None was more right in his response to God. Each just wrote whatever the Lord had placed on his heart in an effort to translate his thoughts into actions.

Turning Your Bible into a Journal

If the thought of having to write in a journal leaves you feeling paralyzed, there are simpler ways to use writing to respond to God. Instead of buying an intimidating journal of unending blank pages, invest instead in a great highlighter, a good pen, and a pack of Post-it notes.

Sometimes journaling can be as simple as highlighting a verse in your Bible. When you highlight a verse, it suddenly becomes yours. No longer is it just a random passage buried in an overwhelming library of conversation. Instead, it becomes a personal message whispered directly into your ear by the Holy Spirit.

Other times, all you may want to do is write something short and simple in the margins of your Bible. Maybe it's "Me too" next to one of David's prayers, or "I needed this today" next to one of Jesus's promises. Sometimes you may only write today's date next to a verse as a reminder of how and when God spoke to you.

When a verse is particularly helpful, you may just want to copy it down on a Post-it note, index card, or small piece of paper so that you can refer to it throughout the day. No commentary necessary. Just God's Word in your handwriting as a personal tool for action.

Think outside the Journal

If the whole point of journaling is to process your thoughts so that you can translate them into action, consider that perhaps it's possible for you to process your thoughts in another way to get the same results.

It may be that you feel led to respond creatively, but you're not bent toward writing. Consider other creative outlets instead. You may have artistic abilities and feel led to paint or draw or sculpt a piece of art in response to God's faithfulness to you. Do it! Think of how many amazing works of art we would have been denied if someone had told Leonardo da Vinci or Michelangelo they should write exclusively rather than create art.

Perhaps you have an eye for photography and are drawn to capture God's images through your camera as a result of how God is speaking to you. Click away!

Are you musical? Create music. Are you graceful? Dance! Are you talkative? Engage in meaningful conversations.

Any of these things can become successful ways of taking God's Word and writing it on your heart so that it results in change in your life.

Of course, it may be that you don't have a creative bone in your body, in which case, that's still perfectly acceptable. Your mind may freeze when you stare at a blank piece of paper, but when you're in the shower, your thoughts are as clear as the water running down the drain. If so, use that time to think about the things of God.

Maybe your mind works best when you're working out. Or baking. Or gardening. Or driving. Don't fight your mental tendencies or try to conform to a random standard of thought processes. Consider how and when you think most clearly and use that outlet to respond to God's Word.

The most eloquent journal in the world is meaningless if it's written by a woman whose life does not reflect obedience to God.

If He's calling you to write, do it. But if He's calling you to stop writing and start living differently for a change, then drop your pen right now and do that instead.

You don't even have to post online about it first.

David's Holy Boogie
2 Samuel 6:12–23

Of all the words recorded in the Bible, David's journal entries stand out among the rest. His ability to put quill to parchment left us with a treasure trove of timeless songs and prayers that often express the deepest cries of our hearts even better than we can ourselves. "The LORD is my shepherd, I lack nothing" (Psalm 23:1). "LORD, our Lord, how majestic is your name in all the earth!" (Psalm 8:9). "Create in me a pure heart, O God, and renew a steadfast spirit within me" (Psalm 51:10). Clearly, David *needed* to process his relationship with the Lord through journaling.

But then came a moment when words were not enough.

In the Old Testament, the ark of the covenant, or ark of the Lord, was a sacred chest of wood and gold built during the time of Moses. Housing artifacts such as the tablets inscribed with the Ten Commandments and the rod of Aaron, the ark was not only a focal point of worship but a tangible representation of God's presence among the Israelites. Imagine their devastation when the ark was stolen by the Philistines when Eli was priest.

Later, when David finally became king, one of his first orders of business was to return the ark of the Lord to its rightful place in Jerusalem. This order was much more significant than simply moving furniture across town. Having the ark back in their possession symbolized an entire nation returning to the Lord. It was a moment of repentance. A moment of revival. A moment of celebration.

Overcome by the weight of it all, David put down his quill and "danc[ed] before the LORD with all his might" (2 Samuel 6:14). He didn't escape to a quiet pasture with his thoughts or retreat to rushing waters with his words. Instead, he tossed off his kingly formal wear, threw a party, and boogied his way down the parade route. It was rambunctious worship at its best.

Later, when chastised by his wife, who preferred a king to stand rather than shimmy, David chose his authentic relationship with his Lord over the superficial expectations of others. He didn't care what others thought. He would respond however the Lord prompted him to, even if it meant becoming "even more undignified than this" (v. 22).

Twist. Dab. Moonwalk. Jive. In those moments when words simply aren't enough, consider letting your body—created by God for His glory—speak for you.

Real Women, Real Stories

Shawnita—Handwriting Method

I learned to speed-read when I was in high school, and it's a skill that helped me in Bible college and as I earned my master's and doctorate in theology. If I wanted, I could blow through an entire chapter of the Bible in a snap, but it does me no good if I'm not slowing down and thinking about what I've read.

A few years ago, a teacher at church encouraged us to write out the Christmas story in Luke, and I found I really enjoyed that process. It forced me to slow down and helped me concentrate on what I was reading. After that, handwriting became a regular part of my quiet time, and I wrote out several stories from the Old Testament and many passages from the New Testament.

Handwriting uses a different section of your brain than when you hear or read something, and the act of physically writing something by hand imprints it differently onto your brain. For me, it's a more permanent imprint.

After some time, I decided I would start at the beginning and write my way through the entire Bible. With a few colored pens, a dozen cheap composition notebooks from Costco, and my childhood King James Version Bible, I opened to Genesis and started writing. Some days I write out an entire chapter of the Bible. Other days I have time for only a few verses. After two-and-a-half years of handwriting regularly during my quiet time, I've made it to Isaiah 51.

I try to keep the process fairly simple because my goal is to focus on the Scriptures themselves, not the act of writing. All of my verses are written in plain black ink. Verse numbers are written in blue. Chapter headings are green. When I finally get to the New Testament, I think I'll write the words of Jesus in red.

Becky—Guided Journaling

I have a "Martha" personality, always busy and always on the go, so I struggle with being easily distracted during my quiet times with the Lord. But since I became a widow a year ago, I have discovered that I am less likely to be distracted if I'm journaling. I've gained comfort, encouragement, and healing from using a grief devotional book, a devotional for women, and a guided prayer journal. It helps to write out my personal and specific prayers, and I stay focused because the journal walks me through different sections such as reflections, thanksgiving, highlights, and what's on my heart. I also listen to instrumental "soaking" music to help me block out the world and focus on God's love, mercy, faithfulness, and blessings. Every now and then, when I'm especially hungry for more in-depth Bible study, I can focus for longer, and my quiet time extends past my usual twenty to thirty minutes.

On the days when my morning routine is otherwise scheduled, I enjoy worship time with the Lord by listening to a variety of gospel music (hymns, choral, and some contemporary) and by engaging in sporadic moments of prayer while in my car between errands. I continue to be amazed and in awe of the many moments that the Holy Spirit comforts and encourages me with just the right Scriptures within His perfect and precious timing! To God be all glory, honor, and praise!

Pat—Journaling Is Frustrating

I have some learning disabilities and have struggled with how long it takes me to get anything accomplished. I also struggle with spelling, so journaling is very frustrating for me. But God has helped me learn not to compare myself with others and to just enjoy life with Him. His grace meets me right where I am, and I do not worry about what others do. I just meet with God.

My time with Him varies from day-to-day. Most mornings, I get up, fix a cup of coffee, and sit in my chair. I'll read a devotion or just a psalm or proverb. Other days, I put in earbuds and go for a walk while listening to Christian music. I get a lot of praying in while I walk.

Another thing that helps me is the phrase "and God . . ." As I go through my day, I pray to God as if I'm having one continuous conversation with Him. Each time I think of something else I want to talk to Him about, I just say, "and God . . ." and pick up where I left off. It helps me keep my focus on Him even though I am busy doing life.

Imogene—First Letters Only

I have one little gimmick I use to help me stay focused as I pray. With a pen and blank piece of paper, I write the first letters of names and requests. For example, I might write JW, meaning, "Please help Jack find a godly wife." I don't save the list because I probably couldn't remember what it meant later if I wanted to. It just helps my mind not to wander as I pray. I wish my method was more dramatic than that, but it's the simplicity that helps me most.

Sue—Greeting God

My tendency is to open my Bible and immediately jump into study mode. I like analyzing. I like asking hard questions. I like digging deep into the Word with charts and outlines and diagrams and bullet points. I am both a student of the Bible and a teacher of the Bible.

But when I want to spend intimate time with God in my quiet time, I have to put all that aside. I have to turn off my analytical brain and focus on *who* I'm talking to. My husband calls this greeting God. So when I sit down to spend time with Him, I start by greeting Him and acknowledging who He is. He is my Lord. My Savior. And it is an *honor* to communicate with Him. When I show up, He's there, waiting for me. He reminds me who He is and how I'm supposed to respond to Him.

If something comes to mind that I want to study more deeply later, I jot it down so I won't forget it. This keeps me from chasing tangents and losing focus so I can keep my attention on the Lord.

Kay—Ebenezer Stone

Years ago, my grandson was trying to skip rocks and accidentally chipped a pot I had on my front porch with one of the rocks. When I picked up the rock, I discovered how perfectly it fit into the palm of my hand, like it was made just for me.

I had recently read in 1 Samuel 7 about how the Lord helped the Israelites gain victory over the Philistines. To remember what God had done, Samuel took a stone and named it *Ebenezer*, which means "stone of help."

I took that random rock and made it my own Ebenezer stone. I hold it in my hand at night when I pray, and it reminds me that God helps me. Many mornings, I wake up and find it buried in the covers beside me. Again I remember, God helps me. He's helped me in the past, and He will continue to help me in the future.

Guilt-Free Ideas for More

1. Paint a picture based on your favorite Bible verse.

2. Pick a meaningful verse or passage and write it on twenty-five different Post-it notes or index cards. Hide them around your home or office, and watch as God allows you to find them at just the right time.

3. Find twenty things around your home that you're thankful for, and take a picture of them.

4. Write out the words to your favorite hymn.

5. Write God a thank-you note.

6. List at least twenty words that describe God. Create a word cloud on wordclouds.com, and print it as a reminder of who God is.

7. Diagram the sentences in your favorite passages. Reflect on how the grammar enhances the meaning.

8. Sketch out your favorite Bible story like a comic strip.

9. Buy colorful pens and highlighters to mark up your Bible as the Lord speaks to you through Scripture.

10. Respond to God's Word by painting rocks. Keep them in your garden as a reminder of your time with Him, or place them in the community to be a blessing to others.

Reflect and Discuss

1. Did you ever keep a diary as a child? If so, what did you write about in it?
2. Have you ever journaled during your quiet time because you felt you had to, rather than because you wanted to?
3. How do you feel about writing in your Bible?
4. How do you best process your thoughts in order to translate them into actions?
5. What creative outlet might you try in lieu of, or in addition to, journaling?

Your Quiet Time Must Be in the Same Place Every Day

Location, location, location! There are only a handful of proper locations to have your quiet time. They include the biblical classics such as on a mountainside, in a garden, in a fishing boat, in a prayer closet, or in the wilderness. If you find yourself in a lions' den or a fiery furnace, that may be acceptable too, but just the one time. Above all, however, the location must be kept a secret because if someone sees you having your quiet time, you're just showing off. Become like Superman and mysteriously disappear for long periods of time each day. If you must create an alter ego to explain your absence, the journalist thing worked for him, so it might work for you as well.

TRUTH: God will meet with you regardless of where you are.

God in the Fog

It sounded like a good idea at the time. A Friday night youth event at church called 5th Quarter where students from area high schools would meet up in one central location after the local football games and hang out until midnight. My teenage son, who had zero interest in actually attending a football game, jumped at the idea of an after-party and convinced me to take him and his friends.

We loaded up the car at an hour I usually reserved for bedtime and drove up the freeway to church, where a row of cars lined the entrance and unloaded cars full of teenagers. Before I could say, "Make good choices!" my boys had already bolted out of the car and slammed the doors behind them, leaving me with three hours to kill before pickup time.

I circled the parking lot, weighing my options. If I went home,

I would most likely fall asleep. If I sat in my car reading, I would most likely fall asleep. On the edge of campus, flood lights shone through the foggy October night and illuminated the green space that surrounded our large, white campus cross that now seemed to glow in the night like a lighted invitation. I had my answer.

A quick search through my messy car unearthed treasures galore. Snacks. A water bottle. My married-name-on-the-cover physical Bible (how'd that get in here?). And, drumroll please, a sleeping bag! It was as if Jesus himself had planned this moment for us.

I spread out beside the cross, cocooning myself in the sleeping bag with the flood lights illuminating my Bible, and spent the entire evening praying, listening, reading, and watching the air particles float in the fog as if worshiping God with dance.

Behind me, the freeway was alive with cars and trucks that zipped and zoomed and zigzagged ribbons of red and white light behind them. A hundred yards to my right, hundreds of teens played and partied with the energy of ants at a summer picnic.

But in that moment, in my quiet corner of the universe, my soul was at rest with God in the fog.

In fact, as King David reminds us in Psalm 139, there's nowhere we can go to escape His presence:

> Where can I go from your Spirit?
> > Where can I flee from your presence?
> If I go up to the heavens, you are there;
> > if I make my bed in the depths, you are
> > > there.
> If I rise on the wings of the dawn,
> > if I settle on the far side of the sea,
> even there your hand will guide me,
> > your right hand will hold me fast.
> If I say, "Surely the darkness will hide me
> > and the light become night around me,"

even the darkness will not be dark to you;
the night will shine like the day,
for darkness is as light to you.

Psalm 139:7–12

Where Are You Now?

It is true that some locations inspire intimacy more than others. For you, it may be that the sights, sounds, and smells of the secluded path near your home evoke feelings of closeness with God that you've been unable to recreate elsewhere. Perhaps you have a vacation home in the mountains that draws you to the Lord with the crisp weather and serene views. Or maybe it's simply that you're most comfortable at your kitchen table with your Bible and a cup of coffee.

Intimate locations can inspire intimacy, but intimate moments can also be fostered in other locations as well.

If you don't have a private room in your home or a tranquil lake outside your back door, it doesn't mean that you can't develop a great place to spend time with God.

In the Bible, Jesus often withdrew to the mountains to meet with God. Moses did too. David had the quiet pastures of his sheep to explore, and Adam and Eve had the perfect garden.

But God also met with Paul and Silas in prison. He stood with Daniel in the lions' den. He met with Shadrach, Meshach, and Abednego in the middle of a fiery furnace. And He met with Samson in a temple crowded with Philistines.

Matthew was sitting at a tax collector's booth when Jesus spoke to him. A man with leprosy was healed in the middle of a crowd of people. And a thief cried out to Jesus as they both hung dying on crosses.

God does not communicate with you based on real estate. He doesn't sit behind a cartoon lemonade stand like Lucy from the Peanuts gang and wait for you to come to Him during office hours for five-cent "psychiatric help." He wants to meet with you regardless of where you are, and He will always come to you.

Are you in the hospital? God is there. Are you in a teacher's lounge? God is there. Are you in your car? In the shower? On the subway? On a ski lift? In your laundry room? In prison? Waiting in line? On an airplane? At the gym? At a bar? On the mission field? In your garden?

God goes to all of those places too.

What Is a Prayer Closet, and Do You Need One?

A prayer closet is a term you might hear to describe a specific place someone sets aside in order to pray, read her Bible, or simply focus on God without distractions. The term originated from the King James Version of Matthew 6:6: "But thou, when thou prayest, enter into thy closet, and when thou hast shut thy door, pray to thy Father which is in secret; and thy Father which seeth in secret shall reward thee openly."

Before you insist that you need to hire a contractor to build an extra room onto your home that mirrors Oprah's meditation room, consider the context in which Jesus was speaking when He said, "Enter into thy closet." He was cautioning against hypocrisy, warning us not to become like the Pharisees who turned prayers into performances. The motivation for their "quiet times" was a desire to be seen by others, not a desire to meet with God.

If you want a special "prayer closet" so you can point it out to your friends when they come to your house for monthly game night, then you have become no different than the hypocrites who prayed out in the open so that others could see them. If, however, you want a "prayer closet" because you desire a specific place set aside for meeting with God, then feel free to create that space however you wish. The issue is not the location itself; it's the motivation behind the location.

Consider a Change of Scenery

I don't know about you, but I wouldn't want to go to the same restaurant every evening for supper, even if I ordered something new every night. I wouldn't want to go to the same resort every summer for vacation either. And I wouldn't even want to look at the same curtains hanging in my bedroom every day for the next thirty years.

But for some reason, we often think that variety is acceptable and encouraged in every area of our lives except for our quiet times. In those cases, variety means inconsistency.

The truth is that too much routine can sometimes cause your time with the Lord to become a ritual rather than a conversation. It may be that if your quiet times have become stale, stagnant, or just plain boring, you simply need a change of scenery.

If you're always indoors when you read your Bible, go outside for a change. If you're always outside, go inside. Create time with the Lord in a variety of settings and situations and see how it heightens your ability to hear Him speak.

I remember one beautiful spring day in college when one of my English professors stopped class right in the middle of her lecture and declared that the day was too beautiful for us to be stuck inside with our noses in our books. So rather than continue with our current lessons, we all walked outside, picked a shady spot under some trees, and listened as she read poetry to us for an hour.

Just that simple change of scenery made an impact on me that I haven't forgotten in over twenty years.

Likewise, I can remember specific times when God spontaneously called me out of my routine and into new and exciting locations to meet with Him. I remember sneaking into the chapel at my local YMCA and reading my Bible instead of exercising. I remember making my husband pull over on the side of a desolate highway in Arizona when I spotted a tiny church with an invitation to "Pause. Rest. Worship." I remember throwing my head back in the air and swinging on the swings at a park when I was overcome with God's blessings. And I remember going back to those same swings and crying out to Him in anguish after finding out I'd had a miscarriage.

Sometimes, if you're going through a difficult time and need to pour out your innermost thoughts to the Lord, you may need a perfectly staged, traditional prayer-closet type of setting to do so. Other times, you may have intellectual struggles with doctrine or God's will, and you'd be better suited to gather your Bible and computer and hole up in a corner of your local library instead.

Is God calling you away from your kitchen table? Is He asking you to get up from your favorite recliner? He may want you to go into your backyard for an hour or to Haiti for an entire month. Follow Him. See what it is He's waiting to show you!

DEVOTIONAL MOMENTS FROM THE BIBLE

Behind Bars with Paul and Silas
Acts 16:13–40

In towns with not enough Jews for a synagogue, it was customary to meet with God at a *proseuche* or open-air gathering place set aside for prayer and worship. In ancient Philippi, Paul and Silas discovered a *proseuche* at a riverside outside the city gates and went there to meet with God on the Sabbath.

The location was ripe with potential. Peaceful. Intimate. Rushing water for washing their hands before prayer. On their first visit, they met a woman named Lydia who became the first convert to Christianity in Europe. After baptizing her and her whole family, they couldn't wait to return to their special place of prayer.

Unfortunately, they wound up in prison instead.

On their way to the *proseuche*, a slave girl possessed by an evil spirit began disturbing them. When Paul ordered the spirit to leave the girl, her owners were outraged because they had been profiting from her fortune-telling abilities. They dragged Paul and Silas to the Roman authorities who threw them in jail.

At once, their plans for a perfect place of prayer were crushed. Ripped from the sunlight, beaten with rods, and tossed into the darkness of the inner prison, they found their feet fastened in stocks when they should have been soaking in a stream.

Rather than wallow in the nightmare of their horrific setting, Paul and Silas chose to create a *proseuche* right where they were—behind prison bars and all. Prayer. Hymns. Worship. All while the other prisoners watched and wondered. Unfazed by their change in location, God blessed their impromptu midnight moment and turned their sweet, intimate time with Him into a full-fledged revival.

In the middle of their singing, an earthquake shook the prison so violently that all the doors flew open and everyone's chains came undone. Paul and Silas could have fled. Finally free from the shackles and bars, they could have returned to the river and left the dark, dank dungeon behind. But they and the others remained.

When the jailer realized that none of the prisoners had escaped, he was so touched that he asked Paul and Silas, "Sirs, what must I do to be saved?" (v. 30). That very night, the jailer and his whole family were saved and baptized.

Riverbed or prison bed. Outside or inside. Morning or

midnight. Your own *proseuche* or "place of prayer" can be wherever you are right now.

Real Women, Real Stories

Heather—In the Car

My commute to work is about thirty to forty minutes each way, so my car has become my favorite place for spending time with the Lord. I usually use the Bible app or a sermon series I've been listening to, but it varies every day. Sometimes I listen to a Christian book or worship music. Other times, I drive in silence and use that time to pray. My only criteria is that my time in the car brings me into a closer relationship with Christ.

The weekends are a little more difficult because I don't have that dedicated time in my car during my commute, so those two days of the week I tend to get a little distracted. But mostly, it's five days a week. That's my routine.

Jen—Mountain Hikes

My sanity is dependent on spending time with God outdoors. I am blessed to live in the Rocky Mountains—a place well known for its beauty. When I'm feeling overwhelmed, daily hikes with mountain views can quiet my soul. I also enjoy paddleboarding on pristine lakes near my home or pushing my muscles to summit new peaks because those adventures turn into sweet times of prayer and reflection.

For me, being still is challenging. But I finally learned that being still does not have to mean physically. It can mean mentally as well. When I'm outside in nature, my mind can be still and my soul can be renewed by the peace of God, even while my body is moving and working.

Psalm 121:1–2 says, "I lift up my eyes to the mountains—where does my help come from? My help comes from the LORD, the Maker of heaven and earth." That's literally what I do. I lift my eyes to the mountains to remember how much God loves me. Sometimes I use worship music or devotions to help direct my thoughts, but mostly it's simply being surrounded by God's creation, hiking up the mountains, and recognizing the power of the Lord that impacts my time with God the most.

Gloria—A Personal Prayer Room

I always wished for a dedicated, quiet place in my home where I could be undistracted to read Scripture, pray, and study. It took a long time, but I was finally able to make it happen.

We did a small remodel job on our home several years ago and were able to transform a room that was being used as a library into a prayer room. It has taken my devotion time to another level. I am naturally an early riser, so I wake up every morning between four and four thirty and usually spend about an hour in my prayer room. I use several favorite devotional books and Bible translations. Most recently they have included classic writings by Charles Stanley, Charles Spurgeon, and Billy Graham. I also review the notes I have from my Sunday lessons at church and read from Psalms and Proverbs each day. This prolonged time with God helps reinforce the biblical principles I've tried for a long time to practice in my life.

This routine is part of my life, seven days a week. Then I am ready for gym time and the office.

Nadine—A Secret Place

In the past, I tried routines for my quiet time, and they worked well for a season. But then my work schedule changed, and I started working early, late, *and* night shifts. I couldn't keep up anymore and was frustrated all the time. That season taught me to focus less on keeping a routine and more on finding a secret place with Jesus and just showing up.

Jesus is there—always—no matter when my work or life schedule allows. Some days I come with an agenda. I have things to study or something to find out. I come with questions, worries, things to talk about. Other days I just sit there and make myself available.

Sometimes I can't concentrate. I'm too tired to talk or—every once in a while—I'm just pouty. I still show up. I show up and share life. That's friendship.

Yes, sometimes the Holy Spirit reminds me that I haven't used all of my spiritual tools and asks me to get a little more diligent in some areas. They're not called spiritual disciplines for no reason. On the other hand, guilt has never opened the door into a great quiet time for me.

The real game changer was finding a secret hideaway spot in my house adorned with a favorite carpet in my guest room and recreating that spot in my mind. I imagine a place that nobody else has access to. I don't invite anyone else in but Jesus. It's where I can imagine sitting with Jesus at the fireplace and just *be*.

Lexi—A Plan and a Partner

My quiet time with the Lord happens either at my kitchen table or at the corner spot on my couch. I either read a few chapters of the Bible or do a specific Bible study. For the past few years, I've been using a chronological Bible reading plan. Sometimes I pause it for other church Bible studies, but I always want some kind of plan in place so I don't have the excuse of defaulting to nothing or not being focused in study. I also have a friend who I read through the Bible with each year. We track together on the Bible app and can make comments to each other. The accountability makes such a difference.

I am a mom of two small children, so I strive to wake up before them to have my Bible study and prayer time. If it doesn't happen in the morning, then I do it in the afternoon as the children have their nap or quiet time. I have been convicted recently that if I have any spare time in the day, it needs to be in God's Word. Housework and other tasks can wait.

Andie—Out to the Pasture

I've been using various psalms to express what's in my heart over the last few months. When David was younger, he had to spend time with his sheep for them to form the relationship they had. In the same way, I need to spend time with God to form a relationship with Him.

When I need to rest in God's presence, I go out to the pasture—a literal pasture, just like David's. We have a small homestead with a small herd of goats, so I go and sit with the does in their pen. I am their goatherd. They know me and I know them. I recognize each doe and call her by name. I know which doe needs to come and sniff my hand and hold it out to her as an invitation. In return, they come to me and get close to me. They've come to know me by my voice, my whistle, and even my smell.

Whenever I am with them, it reminds me how I need to yield myself to our great Shepherd. Most of the time I talk out loud to God, but the last couple of times, I have begun singing love songs of worship to Him. These songs calm me, and in those moments, I'm reminded to humble myself before God. I want to be close to Him. To know His voice. His presence. His blessings. So I continue to go out to the pasture, no matter the season. Even in the Midwest winter, I still spend time with the does in a barn or shelter. My time with them is my time with my Shepherd.

Anne—Exercising with Jesus

I am a busy teacher, wife, and mother of four, so finding quiet time for Jesus can be challenging during the workweek. But, as a teacher, I have become rather good at multitasking, so I combine my quiet time with my exercise time.

In the past, I totally neglected exercise, but this year I set aside time each day to walk on the treadmill. I know there are a lot of people who enjoy exercising, but I am not one of those people. Running, jogging, and walking are not anything I look forward to. However, I decided to make it more positive by exercising with Jesus! Now, each day I look forward to getting on my treadmill because, for me, it is time alone with Jesus. Some days I listen to a podcast, some days I rewatch a sermon on YouTube, and other days I crank up the praise and worship music as loud as Alexa will let me. Exercising is now something I look forward to. I guess Jesus knew that I needed Him to get through it.

Guilt-Free Ideas for More

1. Go to your local library and meet with God in a cubicle.
2. Visit a national park and examine every scenic view as evidence of God's creativity. Tell Him what part of creation amazes you the most.
3. Drive around your neighborhood and pray for your neighbors.
4. Sit on the floor of your closet and pray.
5. Get up high. Go to a skyscraper, a mountain, a Ferris wheel, or something similar and see how your perspective changes. Thank God that He can see things that you cannot.
6. Go for a walk or jog and talk to God during that time.
7. Go snorkeling or scuba diving and discover yet another world God has created.
8. Do a prayer walk through your home, dedicating each room to the Lord as you go.
9. Walk through a cemetery on Easter morning. Reflect on the resurrection of Jesus and its impact on your life.
10. Sit on your front or back porch at dusk and talk to God about your day.

Reflect and Discuss

1. Would you consider yourself an indoor girl or an outdoor girl?
2. Do you function best when the space around you is neat, organized, and tidy or when you're free to stretch out, make a mess, and let your creativity run wild?
3. Where do you typically spend time with God? How does this location work for you?
4. Where have you felt closest to God? Describe a time when a particular place has inspired or intensified your intimacy with Him.
5. How might your relationship with God benefit from a change of scenery? Where might you go?

Conclusion

The Element of Sacrifice

There is one final statement that must be judged as myth or truth: *Your quiet time must contain an element of sacrifice.*

In this case, it's 100 percent true.

My fear, from the first moment I started writing this book, was that exposing all of the legalistic myths associated with quiet times would give the impression that it's going to be easy. Or that it *should* be easy. Or that if it's not easy, it's fine to put it off until it is easy.

But that's not the case.

Your time with God can and should come at a cost. There are things that you must give up. There are luxuries you must sacrifice. There are pieces of yourself that must be set aside.

Effortless is not, and never will be, the goal.

The goal, rather, is to find that energizing zone where your "have to" becomes your "want to," and where you're motivated by desire rather than obligation. This gray middle ground can't be neatly defined or described because it's different for everyone. But you'll know you've found it when you realize that your time with the Lord contains an element of sacrifice, but that the sacrifice is oh- so- worth- it.

The Cost of Sacrifice

There is a lesson about sacrifice to be learned from, of all things, the purchase of some land in 2 Samuel 24. King David wanted to buy the threshing floor of Araunah the Jebusite so he could build an altar to the Lord. When he approached Araunah, Araunah offered to give him the threshing floor free of charge, plus all the oxen, wood, and wheat that he needs. But David refused to accept anything without paying full price. He insisted, "I will not sacrifice to the LORD my God burnt offerings that cost me nothing" (2 Samuel 24:24).

When you strip away the obligations, legalism, and guilt, are you left with a sigh or a battle cry? The first says, "Great! I'm so glad I don't have to spend as much time with God as I thought I did." But the second screams, "But I still *want* to spend as much time as possible with Him! What more can I do to make this happen?"

David knew that his sacrifice would mean more to him if it cost him something. Your quiet times are no different. They may cost you time. They may cost you energy. They may cost you rest or entertainment or even money.

But whatever the cost, it is worth the price. Whatever the sacrifice, it is worth the effort. The greater the investment, the greater the benefits.

The Value of Sacrifice

Remember, however, that the cost of sacrifice is different from the value of sacrifice. Something that costs little on the surface can be of extremely great value, and something that costs a lot on the surface can be of very little value.

Jesus taught us this truth when He examined the widow's offering in Mark 12. Many people gave large sums of money, but

Jesus was most touched by a poor widow who gave just a few cents. "This poor widow has put more into the treasury than all the others," He said. "They all gave out of their wealth; but she, out of her poverty" (Mark 12:43–44).

If you're seeking the Lord and you're trying, truly trying, to grow in Him, do not be discouraged if it still seems like it's not enough. You cannot give what you do not have.

Anyone can spend hours and hours with God when time is not an issue. But when you're down to your last five minutes and you choose to spend them all with Him, He is blessed by that. Are you giving Him the pieces of you that are easy to give? Or are you giving Him the pieces that are difficult to let go of?

When you give all that you have to give, even though it may not seem like much on the surface, God looks below the surface and finds your sacrifice priceless.

The Spirit of Sacrifice

What do you have to give to Him? You may not have an overflow of minutes. You may not have an abundance of energy. You may not have eloquent words. But there is one thing that you can give Him in whatever situation you're in: your heart.

"My sacrifice, O God, is a broken spirit; a broken and contrite heart you, God, will not despise" (Psalm 51:17).

That's beautiful, isn't it? Giving God the sacrifice of your broken spirit and contrite heart. But, let's be honest; it's not very practical. It's way too abstract; it's hard to measure and who even knows what *contrite* means anyway? (It means "sorry" or "remorseful," by the way.)

So if you're supposed to have the spirit of sacrifice, which God loves, what does that look like when you're paying bills? What does that look like in the grocery store? What does that look like on an everyday, folding-laundry, cooking-supper, busy-woman basis?

It looks like this.

Thirteen things you can give God even when you have nothing to give:

- Your thoughts
- Your attitude
- Your obedience
- Your gratitude
- Your praise
- Your attention
- Your reactions
- Your grudges
- Your tears
- Your questions
- Your respect
- Your worship
- Your trust

What else will you add to the list? Having the spirit of sacrifice means that everything you do, everything you say, and everything you think are poured through a God-shaped filter. You stop arranging your life into compartments and picking and choosing which compartments to invite God to inhabit. You stop clocking in and out of church, in and out of prayer, and in and out of quiet times and instead connect to God like one connects to breath.

The Ultimate Sacrifice

And why do you do all of this?

Because it's worth it.

That's the simplest, most basic statement I can leave you with. It's worth it.

Whatever sacrifice you're making to spend time with God, it's worth it because *He* is worth it. You will never regret the minutes you spend on your knees. You will never wish you had read your Bible less. You will never feel as though you've sacrificed more than you've received.

Jesus defined sacrifice when He died on the cross, and His one sacrifice gave value to all other sacrifices.

He didn't give His life so that you could have pretty quiet times. He gave His life so you could know and be known by God.

Start by giving Him your guilt.

Real Women, Real Stories

Haylie—Just Do It

Quiet-time guilt has found me in a number of ways. In the beginning, I didn't really have a desire to read God's Word. That made me feel extremely guilty as a Christian. Then, when I finally had a desire to have a quiet time but didn't do so very often, I felt guilty for not making the time. Finally, when I started having consistent quiet times, I still felt guilty that I hadn't read enough or that I hadn't fully understood what I read.

I know now to focus on quality over quantity. I don't need to read a lot of chapters of the Bible each day to have a successful quiet time. I can just focus on one verse or short passage each day in order to learn more about God and better understand His Word.

I have also found that just doing it—just jumping in and reading God's Word—has given me a greater desire to spend time with Him. Now I read my Bible in the mornings, usually around six fifteen, in a chair in my bedroom. I may miss a morning here or there, but I'm no longer riddled with guilt, and it's definitely more consistent than it used to be.

Rosemarie—Time with Jesus or the Morning News

I communicate with God throughout the day. Since I am aware that the Lord is always with me, I feel like I have a best friend with me at all times. However, I have found that having a specific time with Him takes planning with no excuses to alter those plans.

The best time for me is first thing in the morning. I take my current devotional book, read the passage for the day, and highlight the thoughts I want to remember. If I have missed doing this for a day or two or sometimes more, I try to catch up.

Actually, I often find myself struggling between visiting with the Lord first thing in the morning and turning on the TV to watch the news. But once I get involved with the news, I rarely have my quiet time that day.

Next month, my Bible study group starts back up at my church, so I know my time with God will expand and improve then.

Brenda—War of Flesh and Spirit

I'm sad to say that when I'm not connected to a Bible study or leading a Bible study group, I find it hard to faithfully have a quiet time. Being a preacher's kid and involved in church my whole life, I know better! I know I'm missing that personal time with Jesus and not letting the Holy Spirit lead me into a deeper understanding of Scripture. I know it's my loss when I let life get in the way and become complacent. And I also know it's a war with my flesh and my spirit. I have no excuse!

When I'm winning that war, I spend my time with God in a dedicated study with access to a library of study books and

Bibles. I prefer to use a devotional book or Bible study book to study Scripture. Some of my favorite books are *The One Year Book of Hymns* or *Then Sings My Soul*. I use them to discover the history of hymns, the authors who wrote them, and the background behind their words and music. It encourages me to understand how some of these great Christians lived and served the Lord. With my fresh understanding, I also sing the hymn in worship.

Sadly, the struggles don't go away. I still falter, especially with my prayer life. I am hoping I can be more dedicated with daily Bible study and prayer this year.

Andrea—Honesty above All

One thing I have found is that God simply wants my attention. He's not picky about the way He gets it. So my quiet times change often and rarely look the same.

Sometimes I sing worship music and let the words truly speak to me. I use the lyrics as prayers back to Jesus. Other times I sit quietly in my special chair with my Bible and a cup of coffee. I journal my thoughts about what I read and how I'm feeling at that moment. Sometimes I go through a book study or Bible lesson for my small group, so it's structured and planned out for me. Other times, I simply talk to the Lord in the car about what my heart needs to say.

The only element that remains steady throughout all of my time with God is honesty. It's the most important thing for me that I remain honest with God and tell Him exactly how I feel and what I'm afraid of. He *always* comes through with Scripture, songs, a text from a friend, or a stir in my spirit to alleviate my fears.

I have only had one question not answered: Why? But my heart has learned that the answer doesn't matter, so instead I ask:

What? What are you teaching me? What can I do to honor you? What is true? What *feels* true, but is actually a lie?

I just spend time with God like I do my best friend. He doesn't care how I come, just that I come and trust Him with everything I hold dear. He is trustworthy to hold it for me.

Reflect and Discuss

1. Do you think you have been sacrificing out of your excess or out of your poverty? Why?
2. What sacrifices is God calling you to make in order to deepen your relationship with Him?
3. Which myth do you find hardest to let go of?
4. What is the one thing that spoke to you the most in this book?
5. What is one thing you'll do differently as a result of reading this book?

Acknowledgments

Many thanks to . . .

My Lord and Savior, Jesus Christ, for loving me when I'm unlovable and forgiving me when I'm prone to wander. Have I told you lately how grateful I am for your grace? I love you, and I pray you'll never stop using me for your glory.

My husband, Jason, for following Jesus, leading our family, and being the hardest worker I know. You see me at my worst and encourage me to be my best. I love you, and I love our life together.

My children—Gideon, Canaan, Adelle, and Solomon—for making me laugh, keeping me humble, and being brave enough to challenge me when I fail to live like Jesus. You may all be taller than me now, but you'll never stop being my babies. I love you so much, but Jesus loves you even more. Spend as much time with Him as you can now, while you are young. Nothing matters more.

My sister, Meghan, for holding me accountable and keeping me sane. You always know just how to respond to my texts, phone calls, or sideways glances in crowded spaces. I love you, and I seriously don't know what I'd do without you.

My Priority Ministries sisters—Laurie, Shanda, and Stephanie—for letting me go while never letting go of me. And Pam, for sitting with me for hours as we pored over the first version of this book over a decade ago, and for sitting now at the feet of Jesus in heaven and keeping our work together going strong. I'm convinced this is because of you.

My agent, Cynthia Ruchti, for your never-ending supply of patience, prayers, and godly wisdom. I am so thankful God brought you into my life.

My editors, Dawn Anderson, Katara Patton, and Anna Haggard, and countless others behind the scenes at Our Daily Bread Publishing and God Hears Her. For every detail that goes unseen and unacknowledged, thank you.

My students, both former and current, for strengthening my prayer life. Congratulations, you discovered my life outside the classroom—I write books about Jesus. Now I'll tell you what I couldn't tell you at school—Jesus loves you, and He wants a relationship with you. Yes, I'd love to hear from you. And yes, I'll pray for you or with you any time.

Finally, to every woman who shared her struggles and successes in this book—I was the first person blessed by your stories, but I will certainly not be the last. Thank you for your transparency.

Spread the Word
by Doing One Thing.

- Give a copy of this book as a gift.

- Share the QR code link via your social media.

- Write a review of this book on your blog, favorite bookseller's website, or at ODB.org/store.

- Recommend this book to your church, small group, or book club.

Connect with us. 🅵 🅾

Our Daily Bread Publishing
PO Box 3566, Grand Rapids, MI 49501, USA
Email: books@odb.org

Love God. Love Others.

with  Our Daily Bread.

Your gift changes lives.

Connect with us. ⓕ ⓞ

Our Daily Bread Publishing
PO Box 3566, Grand Rapids, MI 49501, USA
Email: books@odb.org

GOD HEARS HER

Seek and she will find